RASCAL

"Dig 'em out, Wowser," I shouted.

In another minute Wowser was making the dirt fly, and Oscar and I were helping in a frenzy of excitement.

"I'll bet it's a fox," I panted hopefully.

"Probably an old woodchuck," Oscar said.

But we couldn't have been more surprised when a furious mother raccoon exploded from her lair screaming her rage and dismay. Wowser nearly fell over backward to avoid the flying claws and slashing little teeth. A moment later the big raccoon had raked her way up a slender oak tree. Thirty feet above us she continued to scream and scold.

In plain sight now, within the den, we found four baby raccoons, a month old perhaps . . . . Three of the little raccoons, hearing their mother's call, trundled with amazing swiftness into the hazel brush to follow her, and were gone. Oscar, however, was quick enough to cup one kit in his cap, our only reward for our labor—but reward enough, as time would prove.

RASCAL

Rascal

BY
STERLING NORTH

ILLUSTRATED BY JOHN SCHOENHERR

PUFFIN BOOKS

Puffin Books
Published by the Penguin Group
Penguin Putnam Books for Young Readers,
345 Hudson Street, New York, New York 10014
Penguin Books Ltd, 80 Strand, London WC2R ORL, England
Penguin Books Australia Ltd, Ringwood, Victoria, Australia
Penguin Books Canada Ltd, 10 Alcorn Avenue, Toronto, Ontario, Canada M4V 3B2
Penguin Books (N. Z.) Ltd, 182-190 Wairau Road, Auckland 10, New Zealand

Penguin Books Ltd, Registered Offices: Harmondsworth, Middlesex, England

First published in the United States of America by E.P. Dutton,
a division of Penguin Books USA Inc., 1963
Published in Puffin Books, 1990

40 39 38 37 36 35 34 33

ISBN 0-14-034445-4
Library of Congress catalog card number: 89-69817

All of my friends in this book, both animals and human, were real,
and appear under their rightful names.
A few less lovable characters have been rechristened.   —Sterling North

Printed in the United States of America
Set in Baskerville

*For Gladys, my constant companion
in watching our wilderness world*

CONTENTS

CONTENTS

RASCAL

"A very interesting book could be written about the Raccoon and, with its industrious energy and resourcefulness, it deserves to be elevated to the status of the National Emblem in place of the parasitical, carrion-feeding Bald Eagle."
—Ivan T. Sanderson in *Living Mammals of the World*

I: *May*

IT was in May, 1918, that a new friend and companion came into my life: a character, a personality, and a ring-tailed wonder. He weighed less than one pound when I discovered him, a furry ball of utter dependence and awakening curiosity, unweaned and defenseless. Wowser and I were immediately protective. We would have fought any boy or dog in town who sought to harm him.

Wowser was an exceptionally intelligent and responsible watchdog, guarding our house and lawns and gardens and all my pets. But because of his vast size—one hundred and seventy pounds of muscled grace and elegance—he seldom had to resort to violence. He could shake any dog on the block as a terrier shakes a rat. Wowser never started a fight, but after being challenged, badgered, and insulted, he eventually would turn his worried face and great sad eyes upon his tormentor, and more in sorrow than in anger, grab the intruder by the scruff of the neck, and toss him into the gutter.

Wowser was an affectionate, perpetually hungry Saint Bernard. Like most dogs of his breed he drooled a little. In the house he had to lie with his muzzle on a bath towel, his eyes downcast as though in slight disgrace. Pat Delaney, a saloonkeeper who lived a couple of blocks up the street, said that Saint Bernards drool for the best of all possible reasons. He explained that in the Alps these noble dogs set forth every winter day, with little kegs of brandy strapped beneath their chins, to rescue wayfarers lost in the snowdrifts. Generations of carrying the brandy, of which they have never tasted so much as a blessed drop, have made them so thirsty that they continuously drool. The trait had now become hereditary, Pat said, and whole litters of bright and thirsty little Saint Bernards are born drooling for brandy.

On this pleasant afternoon in May, Wowser and I started up First Street toward Crescent Drive where a semicircle of late Victorian houses enjoyed a hilltop view. Northward lay miles of meadows, groves of trees, a winding stream, and the best duck and muskrat marsh in Rock County. As we turned down a country lane past Bardeen's orchard and vineyard, the signature of spring was everywhere: violets and anemones in the grass; the apple trees in promising bud along the bough.

Ahead lay some of the most productive walnut and hickory trees I had ever looted, a good swimming hole in the creek, and, in one bit of forest, a real curiosity—a phosphorescent stump which gleamed at night with fox-

fire, as luminescent as all the lightning bugs in the world
—ghostly and terrifying to boys who saw it for the first
time. It scared me witless as I came home one evening
from fishing. So I made it a point to bring my friends
that way on other evenings, not wishing to be selfish
about my pleasures.

Oscar Sunderland saw me as I passed his bleak farmhouse far down that lane. He was a friend of mine who
knew enough not to talk when we went fishing. And we
were trapping partners on the marsh. His mother was a
gentle Norwegian woman who spoke English with no
trace of an accent, and also her native language. His father Herman Sunderland was another kettle of hasenpfef-
fer—German on his mother's side and Swedish on his
father's—with a temper and dialect all his own.

Oscar's mother baked delicious Norwegian pastries,
particularly around Christmastime. Sometimes in placing
before me a plate of her delicacies she would say something tender to me in Norwegian. I always turned away
to hide the shameful moisture in my eyes. As Mrs. Sunderland knew, my mother had died when I was seven, and
I think that was why she was especially kind to me.

Oscar's tough old father presented no such problem. I
doubt that he had ever said anything kind to anyone in
his life. Oscar was very much afraid of him and risked a
whipping if he were not at home in time to help with the
milking.

No one was concerned about the hours I kept. I was a
very competent eleven-year-old. If I came home long
after dark, my father would merely look up from his

book to greet me vaguely and courteously. He allowed me to live my own life, keep pet skunks and woodchucks in the back yard and the barn, pamper my tame crow, my many cats, and my faithful Saint Bernard. He even let me build my eighteen-foot canoe in the living room. I had not entirely completed the framework, so it would take another year at least. When we had visitors, they sat in the easy chairs surrounding the canoe, or skirted the prow to reach the great shelves of books we were continuously lending. We lived alone and liked it, cooked and cleaned in our own fashion, and paid little attention to indignant housewives who told my father that this was no way to bring up a child.

My father agreed amiably that this might well be true, and then returned to his endless research for a novel concerning the Fox and Winnebago Indians, which for some reason was never published.

"I'm headed for Wentworth's woods," I told Oscar, "and I may not start home before moonrise."

"Wait a minute," Oscar said. "We'll need something to eat."

He returned so swiftly with a paper sack filled with coffee cake and cookies that I knew he had swiped them.

"You'll get a licking when you get home."

"Ishkabibble, I should worry!" Oscar said, a happy grin spreading across his wide face.

We crossed the creek on the steppingstones below the dam. Pickerel were making their seasonal run up the stream, and we nearly caught one with our hands as he snaked his way between the stones. Kildeer started up from the marshy shallows, crying "kildeer, kildeer" as though a storm were brewing.

Wowser had many virtues, but he was not a hunting dog. So we were much surprised when in Wentworth's woods he came to a virtual point. Oscar and I waited silently while the Saint Bernard, on his great paws, padded softly to the hollow base of a rotten stump. He sniffed the hole critically, then turned and whined, telling us plainly that something lived in that den.

"Dig 'em out, Wowser," I shouted.

"He won't dig," Oscar predicted. "He's too lazy."

"You just watch," I said loyally. But I wasn't betting any glass marbles.

In another minute Wowser was making the dirt fly, and Oscar and I were helping in a frenzy of excitement. We scooped the soft earth with our hands, and used our pocket knives when we came to old decaying roots.

"I'll bet it's a fox," I panted hopefully.

"Probably an old woodchuck," Oscar said.

But we couldn't have been more surprised when a furious mother raccoon exploded from her lair screaming her rage and dismay. Wowser nearly fell over backward to avoid the flying claws and slashing little teeth. A moment later the big raccoon had racked her way up a slender oak tree. Thirty feet above us she continued to scream and scold.

In plain sight now, within the den, we found four baby raccoons, a month old perhaps. The entire litter of kits might easily have fitted within my cap. Each tail had five black rings. Each small face had a sharp black mask. Eight bright eyes peered up at us, filled with wonder and worry. And from four inquiring little mouths came whimpered questions.

"Good old Wowser," I said.

"That's a pretty good dog you've got there," Oscar admitted, "but you'd better hold him back."

"He wouldn't hurt them; he takes care of all my pets."

In fact the big dog settled down with a sigh of satisfaction, as near to the nest as possible, ready to adopt one or all of these interesting little creatures. But there was one service he could not render. He could not feed them.

"We can't take them home without their mother," I told Oscar. "They're too young."

"How do we catch the mother?" Oscar asked.

"We draw straws."

"And then what?"

"The one who gets the short straw shinnies up the tree and catches her."

"Oh, no," Oscar said. "Oh no you don't. I ain't that crazy."

"Come on, Oscar."

"No siree."

But at just this moment the four little raccoons set up such a plaintive quavering that we all felt miserable. We *had* to catch that mother raccoon. Wowser was as sad as I was. He pointed his big muzzle toward the evening sky and howled mournfully.

"Well," Oscar said, kicking his shoe into the fresh

earth, "I'd better be getting home to help with the milking."

"Quitter," I taunted.

"Who's a quitter?"

"You're a quitter."

"Well, OK, I'll draw straws; but I think you're loony."

I held the straws and Oscar drew the long one. Naturally I had to live up to my bargain. I looked far above me. In the fading glow of the sunset there she still was, twenty pounds of ring-tailed dynamite. I patted Wowser as though for the last time and began my tough scramble up that slender trunk.

As I shinnied up the tree, in no great hurry to tangle with the raccoon, I had one piece of good fortune. The full moon began to rise above an eastern hill giving me a little more light for my dangerous maneuver. Far out on the first limb, the outraged animal took a firm stance, facing me, her eyes glowing balefully in the moonlight.

"I'm going to cut off the branch with my jackknife," I told Oscar.

"And then what?"

"You're supposed to catch her when she falls in the hazel brush."

Oscar suggested that I had bats in my belfry. But he took off his corduroy jacket and prepared to throw it over the raccoon in a do-or-die effort for which he had little enthusiasm.

Whittling through two-and-one-half inches of white oak with a fairly dull jackknife is a laborious process, as I soon discovered. I was in a cramped position, holding on with my left hand and hacking away at the wood with my right. And I feared the raccoon might try to rush me when the limb began to break.

The moon rose slowly through the trees as blisters rose slowly on my right hand. But I couldn't weaken now. From far below came the whimpering of the raccoon kits, and an occasional mournful howl from Wowser. Tree toads and frogs in the swamp began their chorus, and a little screech owl, sounding almost like another raccoon, added an eerie tremolo.

"How you coming?" Oscar asked.

"Coming fine. Get ready to catch her."

"Count on me," Oscar said, his voice less convincing than his brave words.

The tasseled limb of the white oak sighed at last, broke with a snap, and drifted down to the hazel brush below.

Oscar tried. I will give him credit for that. He tangled for five seconds with that raccoon, and then retreated with a damaged jacket. Three of the little raccoons, hearing their mother's call, trundled with amazing swiftness into the hazel brush to follow her, and were gone. Oscar, however, was quick enough to cup one kit in his cap, our only reward for our labor—but reward enough, as time would prove. As nearly as we could tell, the handsome, sharply marked little animal was covered only with soft gray underfur, having few of the darker guard hairs which later gleam on the adult raccoon.

He was the only baby raccoon I have ever held in my hands. And as he nestled upward like a quail chick,

22

and nuzzled like a puppy seeking its mother's milk, I was both overwhelmed with the ecstasy of ownership and frightened by the enormous responsibility we had assumed. Wowser romped beside us through the moonlight, often coming to sniff and lick the new pet we had found—this bit of masked mischief which had stolen his heart as well as my own.

"He's yours," Oscar said sadly. "My old man would never let me keep him. He shot a 'coon in the chicken house just a few weeks ago."

"You can come and see him," I suggested.

"Sure, I can come and see him."

We walked in silence for a time, thinking of the injustices of the world that made so few allowances for the nature of raccoons and boys of our age. Then we began talking about all the raccoons we had ever seen, and how we would feed this kit and teach him all the things he would have to learn.

"I seen a raccoon mother once with five kits," Oscar said.

"What were they doing?"

"She was leading them along the edge of the stream. They did everything she did."

"Like what?"

"Feeling around with their front paws hunting for crawdads, I guess."

On the horizon there were flashes of distant lightning and a low rumbling of thunder, sounding like artillery many miles away. It reminded us that the war was still raging in France, and that maybe my brother Herschel was being moved up to the front. I hated to think about that terrible war which had been killing and wounding millions of men ever since the year my mother died. Here we were, safe and remote from the war, and worrying about such small and unimportant things as whether Oscar would get a whipping when he got home, and how to feed and raise a little raccoon.

As we came up the lane toward Sunderland's farmhouse, Oscar began saying, "Ishkabibble, I should worry." But he acted worried to me. When we reached his front yard he dared me and double-dared me to go up and knock on the door. Meanwhile he hid behind a flowering spirea bush and waited to see what might happen.

Oscar was wise to let me do the knocking. Herman Sunderland came storming out, swearing in German and Swedish. He was certainly angry with Oscar, and he didn't seem to like me very much either.

"Vere is dot no-goot son of mine?"

"It wasn't Oscar's fault," I said. "I asked him to come for a walk with me, and . . ."

"Vere iss he now?"

"Well," I said.

"Vell, vell, vell! Vot you mean, vell?"

"We dug out a den of raccoons," I said, "and here is the one we brought home."

"Coons," shouted Sunderland, "*verdammte* varmints."

I was afraid that Mr. Sunderland might flush Oscar from behind the spirea bush, but at just this moment Oscar's gracious mother came out on the front porch, the moonlight shining on her silvering hair.

"Go to bed, Herman," she said quietly. "I will take care of this. Come out, Oscar, from behind that bush."

To my surprise, Oscar's father meekly obeyed, taking a lamp up that long, dark parlor stairway—his shadow much taller than himself. And Oscar's mother took us to the kitchen where she fed us a warm supper and began to heat a little milk to the temperature that would be right for a human baby.

"It is hungry, the little one," she said, petting the small raccoon. "Go fetch a clean wheat straw, Oscar."

She filled her own mouth with warm milk, put the wheat straw between her lips, and slanted the straw down to the mouth of the little raccoon. I watched, fascinated, as my new pet took the straw eagerly and began to nurse.

"Look how the little one eats," Oscar's mother said. "This is the way you will have to feed him, Sterling."

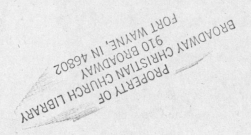

II: *June*

JUNE was the month! School was out, cherries were ripe, and all the boys and some of the girls went barefoot. Boys had many extra advantages such as swimming naked and wandering alone along the streams and rivers, casting for bass among the water lilies. Girls had to wear swimming suits and come in earlier from our evening games of prisoner's base and run-sheep-run. I was very thankful that I was a boy.

Despite mowing lawns and working in my war garden, I had many additional hours to spend with my pets, watching my woodchucks nibbling clover, feeding my four yearling skunks their bread and milk, and trying to keep Poe-the-Crow from stealing bright objects such as car keys. Most satisfying of all were the hours that I spent with my small raccoon whom I had named Rascal.

Perhaps a psychologist might say that I had substituted pets for a family. I had a human family, of course—interesting. well-educated, and affectionate. But Mother was dead, my father often away on business trips, my brother Herschel fighting in France, and my sisters Theo and Jessica now living their adult lives. Both sisters had taken tender care of me after Mother died, Jessica in particular postponing her career and marriage.

But now Theo was happily wed to a young paper-mill owner in northern Minnesota, and Jessica, a talented linguist and poet, was taking postgraduate work at the University of Chicago. Often the only occupant of our ten-room house was an eleven-year-old boy working on his canoe in the living room and thinking "long, long thoughts."

One problem that puzzled me was theological. I asked myself how God could be all-knowing, all-powerful, and all-merciful and still allow so much suffering in the world. In particular, how could He have taken my gifted and gentle mother when she was only forty-seven years old?

I asked some of these questions of Reverend Hooton,* the Methodist minister whose church and parsonage adjoined our property, and his answers were not particularly satisfying.

It seemed to me unfair that she could not have lived to see the pets I was raising—Rascal especially. I could imagine her pleasure both as a biologist and as a mother. She would have been interested in studying more closely

* Father of Earnest A. Hooton, anthropologist and author.

the habits of all these animals, and would have helped me solve some of the difficult problems they presented.

For instance, both my crow and my skunks were currently in trouble with the Methodists. Poe-the-Crow lived in the belfry of the church, and shouted the only phrase he knew, "What fun! What fun!" as dignified parishioners came to church services, weddings, and funerals. There was one faction of the church in favor of evicting Poe, with a shotgun if necessary.

My harmless skunks had further complicated matters on a recent Sunday evening. These pleasant pets that I had dug from a hole the previous spring were now more than a year old and somewhat restless. They were handsome, glossy creatures—one broad-stripe, one narrow-stripe, one short-stripe, and one black beauty with a single star of white on his head. All four had perfect manners. Having never been frightened or abused, they had never scented up the neighborhood.

But one night in June when Wowser must have been drowsing, a stray dog came barking and snarling at them through the woven wire, and they reacted predictably. Sunday services were progressing at the church not seventy feet from their cage. It was a warm evening, and the windows of the choir loft were open. For the first time in his life Reverend Hooton shortened his sermon.

On Monday morning a delegation of deacons came to protest to my father.

With both Poe and the skunks at issue, I was in double jeopardy, so I decided to make an accommodation. I gave all my skunks a last meal of bread and milk and took them in two carrying baskets to Wentworth's woods where there were many empty dens to hide in. The Methodists were so pleased to be rid of the skunks that they decided to postpone indefinitely the eviction of Poe-the-Crow.

Rascal meantime was living in a hole some five feet above the ground in our big red oak tree. Since raccoons usually stay in their nest for the first two months of their lives, I saw little of my pet except when I took him out to feed him. I soon taught him how to drink his warm milk from a saucer, which was a great improvement over the laborious process of letting him nurse through a wheat straw.

Wowser was his guardian, remaining almost constantly at the foot of the oak tree, even sleeping there at night.

But on an afternoon in mid-June, Wowser and I were both alerted by a quavering trill at the hole in the tree, and there we saw a small black mask and two beady eyes peering out at the wide world beyond. A moment later Rascal had executed an about-face and was emerging from the hole, ring tail first, backing down the tree cautiously in the manner of a little bear. Raccoons have five unretractable claws on each of their hands and feet, making headlong descent inadvisable. So Rascal instinctively came down tail first, scrambling frantically from time to time, and often looking over his shoulder to see how far he was from the ground.

Wowser was very much disturbed and yelped a few questions, looking up to see how I felt about this new problem. I told my Saint Bernard not to worry, just to wait and watch.

Rascal must have been surveying the back yard very thoroughly from his front door for he started immediately for my shallow, cemented, bait pond, always alive with minnows.

The edges of this pool slanted gradually toward the deeper central portion, making it convenient for my amazingly confident little raccoon. Without a moment's hesitation he waded in and began feeling all over the bottom, his sensitive prehensile fingers telling him all that he needed to know about this minnow pond. Meanwhile his eyes seemed to focus on the far horizon, as though eyes and hands were in no way connected. Shiners and chubs dashed frantically for safety, sometimes leaping clear of the water in their attempt to escape.

As Rascal methodically circled the pool on his first fishing expedition, I marveled that one so young, and with no mother to teach him, knew precisely the technique used by all other raccoons for catching minnows. I watched fascinated to see if some ancient wisdom stored within his brain would make his search successful. My answer came a moment later when those two clever little black hands seized a four-inch shiner. Then the washing ceremony began. Although the minnow was perfectly clean, Rascal sloshed it back and forth for several minutes before retiring to dry land to enjoy his meal—more delicious because he had caught this fish himself.

Seemingly satisfied with the one minnow, and aware he could catch more any time he wished, Rascal began a leisurely tour of the back yard, sniffing and feeling. There were interesting odors to be classified—odors of cat, dog, woodchuck, and recently evicted skunk. There were crickets in the grass worthy of a pounce, and the chilling shadow of Poe-the-Crow, which for a passing moment froze Rascal in his tracks as a meadow mouse will freeze in the shadow of a hawk.

When Rascal came too near to any of our property lines, Wowser went into action, nudging him back toward the tree. Rascal responded mildly to this discipline, and after another fifteen minutes examining his domain, this small lord of the manor returned to his castle, climbed the tree more easily than he had descended, and disappeared into his hole.

I decided one day that Rascal was clean enough and bright enough to eat with us at the table. I went to the attic and brought down the family highchair, last used during my own infancy.

Next morning while my father was fixing eggs, toast, and coffee, I went out to get Rascal, and placed him in the highchair beside me at the table. On his tray I put a heavy earthenware bowl of warm milk.

Rascal could reach the milk easily by standing in the chair and placing his hands on the edge of the tray. He seemed to like the new arrangement and chirred and trilled his satisfaction. Except for dribbling a little milk, easily wiped from the tray of the highchair, his table manners proved excellent, much better than those of most children. My father was amused and permissive as usual, and even petted the raccoon as we finished our meal.

Breakfast-for-three became part of the daily ritual, and we had no trouble whatsoever until I had the idea of offering Rascal a sugar loaf. It is true we were at war, observing heatless, meatless, and wheatless days, and conserving sugar. But my father and I did no baking, and used almost none of our sugar ration, save for a lump or two in coffee. So I did not feel too unpatriotic when I gave Rascal his first sugar.

Rascal felt it, sniffed it, and then began his usual washing ceremony, swishing it back and forth through his bowl of milk. In a few moments, of course, it melted entirely away, and a more surprised little 'coon you have never seen in your life. He felt all over the bottom of the bowl to see if he had dropped it, then turned over his right hand to assure himself it was empty, then examined his left hand in the same manner. Finally he looked at me and trilled a shrill question: who had stolen his sugar lump?

Recovering from my laughter, I gave him a second sugar lump, which Rascal examined minutely. He started to wash it, but hesitated. A very shrewd look came into his bright black eyes, and instead of washing away a second treat, he took it directly to his mouth where he began to munch it with complete satisfaction. When Rascal had learned a lesson, he had learned it for life. Never again did he wash a lump of sugar.

His intelligence, however, created many problems. For instance, he had seen the source of the sugar—the covered bowl in the middle of the table. And whereas I had previously been able to confine him to his highchair, he

33

now insisted upon walking across the tablecloth, lifting the lid of the sugar bowl, and helping himself to a lump. From that day on, we had to keep the sugar bowl in the corner cupboard to avoid having a small raccoon constantly on the dining room table.

Another lesson he learned swiftly was how to open the back screen door. I purposely had not repaired the catch or replaced the weakened spring, because all of my cats liked to open the door and walk in, or push it from inside and let themselves out again. Rascal watched this performance several times. Obviously the trick was to hook your claws into the screen and pull. Feeling very pleased with himself he showed the cats he was as smart as the oldest and wisest tom.

Several nights later I was startled and delighted to hear Rascal's trill from the pillow beside me, then to feel his little hands working all over my face. My raccoon baby had climbed from his hole, opened the back screen door, and with eyes that could see in the dark had found his way to my bed.

There were no strict rules in our house, as both Rascal and I realized. My raccoon had decided that the very best place to sleep was with me. He was as clean as any cat, housebroken immediately and without training, and he thought my bed was softer and more comfortable than his own in the oak tree. So from that night on we became bedfellows, and for many months we slept together. I felt less lonesome now when my father was away.

Cable stories in the Janesville *Daily Gazette* admitted that the Germans had reached the banks of the Marne and were within sight of the Eiffel Tower. On the big war map in the window of the Tobacco Exchange Bank, the black-headed pins representing the German lines were in several places pushing back the red, white, and blue pins which indicated various allied sectors. Somewhere in that storm of lead and steel my brother Herschel was fighting.

Among my favorite poems at this time were Rupert Brooke's war sonnets and Alan Seeger's prophetic and gallant lament:

> I have a rendezous with Death
> At some disputed barricade . . .

Particularly on nights of thunder and lightning I had nightmares about the war and pulled the covers over our heads. But when the sun arose the next morning to shine upon the rain-wet grass, Rascal and I forgot our fears and prepared to go fishing.

One of my favorite fishing spots was a sand bar below the Indian Ford dam in Rock River—a stream which rises in the Horicon marshes of Wisconsin and enters the Mississippi at Rock Island, Illinois. There were deep holes and rapids, marshy bayous and stretches as quiet as a lake, a beautiful and unpredictable stream.

On a previous evening I had searched the wet lawn with a flashlight to catch more than fifty night crawlers. My jointed steel rod was strapped under the bar of my bicycle, and my tackle box with reel and line and lures was ready to place in the bicycle basket on the handlebars. It was good that my box was small and compact, leaving room for my fishing companion who in the last few days had become a cycling maniac.

Rascal was a demon for speed. Weighing two pounds at most, this absurd and lovable little creature had the heart of a lion. He had learned to stand in the closely woven wire basket with his feet wide apart and his hands firmly gripping the front rim, his small button of a nose pointed straight into the wind, and his ring tail streaming back like the plume of a hunting dog that has come to a point. The most amusing aspect of his racing costume was his natural black goggles around his bright eyes, making him look like Barney Oldfield coming down the home stretch. What he liked best was going full tilt down a steep hill. It worried him slightly when I had to work hard, pumping up the next hill, the front wheel woggling from side to side to keep the bicycle in balance. But as we picked up speed again his confidence returned, and he would peer ahead like the engineer leaning from the cab window of Old Ninety-Nine.

On the southern edge of town we had to pass the cemetery where my mother was buried under a white stone that said:

In Memory of
Sarah Elizabeth Nelson North
1866—1914

It seemed an inadequate tribute, only partially compensated by the roses I had planted there.

From the cemetery it was all downhill to Indian Ford with a fine view of the winding river bordered by woods and pastures and neat, geometric fields of corn, tobacco, wheat, and oats. In these years of war prosperity the barns were newly painted a cheerful red, and the farmhouses white amid wide lawns and flowers. We gained speed in those last two miles, and Rascal came to full attention, the wind sweeping into his face and blowing his whiskers back to his furry ears. We were probably as happy as anyone can be in our world.

This was the first time Rascal had seen Indian Ford, and there were many exciting things to show him: the bridge with girders rising twenty feet above the water from which boys dared each other to dive; the dam itself with a shining sheet of water cascading into the depths below; the powerhouse from which emerged the continuous purring of the dynamos; and finally the swift tailrace, too dangerous for any swimmer, particularly for a small raccoon who had barely learned to dog-paddle.

We turned downriver on a path skirted by willows in which red-wing blackbirds made the day still more liquid with their "Kon-keree! Kon-keree!" And upon a bank overlooking a bend in the big stream we found wild strawberries almost as bright as the red epaulets on the wings of the blackbirds. A single taste of these berries and Rascal waded into the patch snatching and devouring. For one so eager and so curious, each moment brought new delights.

We came at last to my secret fishing place, the sand bar with the deep and quiet hole below it where I had caught more fish than anywhere else in the river. I left my bicycle in the willows and began assembling my jointed pole and reel, running my silk line through the agate eyes and tip, and tying to that line a short gut leader, a swivel, and a red-and-white bass plug.

Rascal needed no such elaborate preparation. His fishing equipment was always ready for immediate use; you might say he was born with more fishing sense and fishing tackle than most human beings acquire in a lifetime.

I watched him for several minutes as he worked his way along the upper edge of the sand bar, examining every inch of the shallows with a slight treading or pumping motion which alternated the pressure and progress of his two hands. His eyes, as usual, played no part in this intimate investigation of his fishing grounds, as his gaze ranged far across the river to the opposite shore. At the outermost point of the bar he was momentarily swept into the stream, and I was preparing to rush to his rescue. But with no apparent distress, he swam back to the quiet water below the bar and began examining this lower margin of the small peninsula.

With the whole river inviting their escape, the minnows were too swift for Rascal's hands. But he soon encountered and grasped a little monster of which he had no previous knowledge.

His catch was a particularly large crayfish (or "crawdad" in the terminology of the region). This fresh-water lobster has claws that can pinch severely, an armored body, and a delicious tail. A feast I had often enjoyed consisted of perhaps twenty-five such crayfish tails boiled over a campfire. Pink, firm, and tasting like shrimp, they furnished an excellent appetizer before the entree of fried catfish or Mulligan stew.

This, however, was Rascal's first crayfish. Had he been informed by his mother, he would have grasped it just behind the claws, thus avoiding any danger from those waving, sawtooth pincers. But having no one to teach him, he missed the safe-and-sane grasp, and was pinched several times before he crushed the head with his needle-sharp teeth, washed his prey, and turned the crayfish around to gobble up the delectable tail.

Once pinched, twice shy. The very next crayfish he caught was handled with the professional skill of an old and wise raccoon.

Feeling certain that Rascal was in no danger from the river, or from its smaller inhabitants, I began my own fishing. I was barefoot, of course, with my overalls rolled high above my knees. So I waded into the cool water at the tip of the point, pleasurably expectant as I prepared for my first cast.

Below the point was cupped the deep, dark pool, edged toward the shore with small pond lilies, water lilies, and slender flowers which we called arrowheads. I cast smoothly toward the hiding place of many a bass and pickerel, reeling in the plug, with pauses to allow any game fish that might be following to strike the lure.

Once a bass struck and missed, but refused to strike again. A few minutes later a sunfish weighing perhaps a pound followed the red-and-white wobbler almost to the end of the pole, then turned in a flash of color and was gone. A dozen more casts produced no additional results, so I reeled in to change my rig for catfish—those big, fighting, fork-tailed silver cats that furnished more sport than any other fish in the river.

Anglers who have never taken this particular mutation of channel catfish find it hard to believe that these fish will strike almost any lure, a buck-tail fly, a live minnow or frog, and of course chicken livers and night crawlers. These trim, slim, and beautiful fish are streamlined for action and will frequently fight for twenty minutes or half an hour before being brought to the net.

As I returned to my tackle box, I saw that Rascal had eaten his fill of crayfish, and had decided to take a nap in the willow shade beside my bicycle. This left me free to give full attention to my fishing.

I attached a bronze catfish hook to my leader, weighted my line with four split buckshot, and strung an appetizing bait of night crawlers on the hook. Once again wading into the water at the point of the sand bar, I cast one hundred feet downstream to the deepest part of the pool. I waited for nearly ten minutes, and then the electrifying moment came. The bait moved twice, the line twitching as the big cat nosed the night crawlers. Then he struck with all his weight, the line singing off the reel as I slowed it with my thumb. As I pulled back to set the hook, my pole bent almost double, and the fight was on.

He tried all of his tricks, once making a long run for the lily pads where he might have tangled the line and broken free, twice making dashes for the faster water where the current could help him. Then for three or four minutes he sulked so deep in the pool I thought he might have gone under a sunken log. He broke water once, all silver and blue, his great forked tail thrashing.

Rascal awoke at this point and trundled over to join in the excitement. As the catfish was reeled in, nearer and nearer to the shore, the raccoon went up and down the sand bar, glancing at me occasionally to ask questions.

"It's a beauty," I told my pet. "One of the best I ever caught."

Rascal extended a tentative paw as I brought it into shallow water, but retreated precipitously when the thrashing tail drenched him. Once I had the fish safely on the sand I slipped my stringer through its gills before I removed the hook. I was taking no last-minute chance of losing this big shining cat, which by the scale in my tackle box weighed just under nine pounds. I tied the stringer to a strong willow root, rebaited, and went back to the point, my heart thumping wildly.

In two hours of fishing I added nothing more to my string except three fat, yellow-bellied bullheads weighing perhaps a pound apiece. However, both Rascal and I went frequently to view again the handsome catfish, tethered to the willow.

It was approaching noon and the fish had stopped biting, so I reeled in, removed my tackle, and unjointed my pole. I put the fish in a gunny sack, crowding Rascal a bit in the bicycle basket, and we started homeward up the river trail, filled with contentment.

At the Fishermen's Rest at Indian Ford I bought a bottle of strawberry pop, and Rascal discovered a new del-

41

icacy. Without so much as a by-your-leave he put one of his little hands into the bottle, licked off his fingers, and began begging. I waited until I had finished all but the last half inch of the bottle, then I poured a few drops into Rascal's open and eager mouth. To my amazement he grasped the neck of the bottle, rolled over on his back, and using both hands and both feet held it in perfect position while he drained the last sweet drops. Strawberry was his favorite flavor from then on. He never did learn to like lemon sour.

All raccoons are attracted by shining objects, and Rascal was no exception. He was fascinated by brass doorknobs, glass marbles, my broken Ingersoll watch, and small coins. I gave him three bright new pennies which he hoarded with the happiness of a little miser. He felt them carefully, smelled them, tasted them, and then hid them in a dark corner with some of his other treasures. One day he decided to carry one of his pennies to the back porch. Poe-the-Crow was perched on the porch rail teasing the cats, but keeping just beyond their reach. This raucous old bird, who cawed and cussed in crow language, was arching his wings and strutting like a poolroom bully as Rascal pushed open the screen and trundled into the sunlight, his penny shining like newly minted gold.

Poe and Rascal had taken an instant dislike to each other when first they met. Crows, like most other birds, know that raccoons steal birds' eggs and sometimes eat fledglings. In addition Poe was jealous. He had seen me

petting and pampering my small raccoon. But Rascal was large enough now to pull a few tail feathers from the big black bird during their noisy squabbles. And Poe, who was no fool, was taking few chances.

The penny, however, was so tempting that the crow threw caution to the winds and made a dive for the bright object (for crows are as insatiably attracted by glittering trinkets as are raccoons, and in addition are inveterate thieves).

Rascal was carrying the penny in his mouth, and when Poe swooped to conquer, his beak closed not only on the penny but upon half a dozen of Rascal's coarse, strong whiskers. When the black thief tried to make his fast getaway he found himself attached to the raccoon, who with a high scream of fury began fighting for his property and his life. Such a tangle of shining black feathers and furious fur you have seldom seen as Rascal and Poe wrestled and struggled. I arrived to untangle them, and both were angry with me. Rascal nipped me slightly for the first time, and Poe made several ungracious comments.

The penny, meanwhile, had rolled from the porch into the grass below, where the crow promptly spotted it, seized it once again, and took wing. "Straight as a crow flies" seldom applied to my wily pet. After any thievery he would travel by devious routes before slipping between the wide slats of the Methodist belfry where he presumably stored his loot.

I gave the incident no more thought, pacified Rascal with another penny, and resumed work on my canoe in the living room.

The blueprint I had made in the manual training shop at school called for a trim and streamlined craft, eighteen feet long and twenty-eight inches wide. The slender longitudinal ribs were fastened at prow and stern and curved around cross-sectional forms between. These and the inner keel were now in place. But the ribs to encircle the craft from gunwale to gunwale presented a problem. I had tried steaming hickory for this purpose, and curving the wood under pressure, but had given it up as an impossible job with my limited equipment.

Then a happy thought struck me. Nothing is tougher than the water elm used in making cheese boxes. An additional convenience is the fact that these cylinders of thin wood are already curved into a complete circle. Most of the tradesmen were friends of mine. They bought the neatly tied bunches of white-tipped, crimson radishes which I raised in my war garden, and gave me meat scraps and stale loaves of bread for Wowser. I was sure they would give me empty cheese boxes if I asked politely.

At Pringle's they had one good cheese box and at Wilson's grocery another. Before I had visited half the food stores in town I had all I needed. At home in the living room I marked two-inch strips on each of these cylinders, and with my father's best ripsaw began the exacting and exasperating job of cutting the featherweight canoe ribs. Some of the boxes split and were ruined. But with patience I finally sawed the forty-two circles that were required. I found to my great joy that these strips of wood had no tendency to spread, but on the contrary held their circular shape to perfection.

45

All of this work in the living room created some disorder, particularly when I began sandpapering the ribs, starting with number-two sandpaper and finishing with double 0, which is very fine. The wood smoothed to a satin surface, creamy yellow and pleasant to the touch.

I was still sanding the ribs, with Rascal clambering over the unfinished canoe, when a Stutz Bearcat curved up the gravel drive. Out stepped my beautiful sister Theodora Maud (the Maud from Tennyson of course). With her was one of her maids, and Theo had a determined look on her patrician face and a light in her eyes that went well with her mass of auburn hair.

"Theo, Theo!" I shouted happily, running out to embrace her.

"Hello, sonny boy—my, you're all covered with sawdust."

"Well you see, Theo, I'm building a canoe."

"That's nice, but where?"

"In the living room," I said, dropping my eyes.

"Merciful heavens!" Theo said. "Now help Jennie with the luggage, and put it in the downstairs bedroom."

I didn't dare tell Theo that I was sleeping in that room and that Rascal slept there too. I loved this sister but I was slightly in awe of her. She had been kind to me after Mother died, and she would be kind to me again some years later when I was stricken by infantile paralysis. But she was a martinet concerning deportment, dress, housekeeping, and much besides. It was her training that made me jump up like a jack-in-the-box whenever an older person, particularly a lady, entered the room. She dressed me on occasion in such fashionable Norfolk suits and jackets that it took several fist fights to prove I was still one of the gang.

Theo gave the living room one sweeping glance and raised her hands in horror.

"I've never seen such a mess in my life," she said.

"I sweep up the sawdust and shavings every evening."

"Yes, I see them, right there in the fireplace."

"Daddy and I do a good job of batching it," I said defensively.

"Batching it! That's just the trouble," Theo said severely. "Now you get that canoe out of the living room this minute, Sterling."

I had a little of the family's fire, so I replied with a firm and angry refusal. I told Theo we were living exactly the way we wanted to live, and that I would never wear a Norfolk suit or a necktie again except on Sundays.

"You're not too big to spank," Theo said, her lovely eyes flashing.

"You just try."

"Now, Sterling, I've brought Jennie to clean this house from top to bottom. I'll cook some decent food. We'll hire a full-time housekeeper, and we'll get this canoe out of the living room."

"Can't you just leave us alone?" I said mournfully. "Anyhow, you're not my mother."

"Oh, sonny boy," she said, suddenly contrite and fighting back the tears. She came around the end of the canoe and kissed me quite tenderly.

Giving Theo the downstairs bedroom didn't worry *me*.

She always took this big room with its adjoining bath. She said none of the other beds was fit to sleep in.

My difficulty would come in trying to explain all this to Rascal. Raccoons have definite patterns in their minds, and Rascal had decisively chosen the same bed that Theo wanted. He also preferred a room with a bath. Each evening I closed the drain of the big lavatory and left a few inches of water in the basin so that Rascal could get a drink at any time during the night, or perhaps wash a cricket before he ate it. How was I to reveal to this small creature of habit that he was being evicted?

Theo had not seen Rascal until this moment. He had been lying low, watching and listening shrewdly. He may not have been a perfect judge of character, but he reacted with surprising sensitivity to various modulations of voice. He knew when he was being praised or scolded and when people were feeling affectionate or angry. He didn't altogether trust this auburn-haired stranger, although his eyes strayed often to her shining hair.

His virtual invisibility was due to the fact that he was lying on a large jaguar-skin rug which Uncle Justus had sent us from Pará, Brazil. The mounted head had realistic glass eyes which Rascal often fondled and sometimes tried to dislodge. The little raccoon blended perfectly into the handsomely marked pelt of the once-ferocious jungle cat.

When Rascal began to rise from that skin, like the disembodied spirit of the Amazonian jaguar, it startled Theo nearly out of her wits.

"What in the world is *that?*"

48

"That's Rascal, my good little raccoon."

"You mean it lives in the house?"

"Only part of the time."

"Does it bite?"

"Not unless you slap him or scold him."

"Now get that thing right out of here, Sterling."

"Well, all right," I agreed reluctantly, knowing that Rascal could let himself back in any time he pleased.

Rascal spent the rest of the day sleeping in the oak tree, but that night when the moon arose, he backed down his tree, padded to the screen door, opened it with ease, and went confidently to our bedroom and crawled in with Theo. My father and I who were sleeping upstairs were awakened by a blood-curdling yell. We rushed downstairs in our pajamas to find Theo standing on a chair, treed by a complacent little raccoon who sat on the floor below blinking up at this crazy human being who was screeching like a fire siren.

"He always sleeps in this bed," I explained. "He's harmless and perfectly clean."

"You take that horrid little animal out of the house this minute," Theo ordered, "and hook the screen door so it can't possibly get back in."

"Well, OK," I said, "but you're sleeping in Rascal's bed. And he has just as many rights around here as you have."

"Don't be impertinent," Theo said, reassuming her dignity.

A later episode of this visit is worth recalling. Recently married, Theo treasured her engagement ring, a square-cut diamond of perhaps one carat, mounted in white gold. She had misplaced this ring on several occasions. Once we dug up eighty-five feet of sewer, only to find that she had transferred the ring to another purse.

True to form, she again lost her ring. She thought she had left it on the wide rim of the lavatory when she went to bed, and that either it had fallen into the drain or had been stolen. No one in Brailsford Junction ever locked his door. Not within memory had there been a robbery.

We ransacked the house, hunted through the grass and the flower beds, and then made plans for again digging up the sewer. Then a farfetched possibility struck me like a bolt from the blue. Just before dawn on that fateful morning I had heard Rascal and Poe having a terrible fight on the back porch. Before I could shake the sleep from my eyes, the cawing and screaming subsided and I had drowsed off again.

Feeling as keen as a Scotland Yard detective, I began to weave a theory. On this fourth night of Theo's visit I had not hooked the screen door. Rascal apparently had slipped into the house, reached the downstairs bedroom, and wisely chosen not to create another scene. He had decided, however, to have a drink of fresh water from the lavatory, had climbed to the window sill and then to the basin, and found it empty. But joy of joys, there on the rim of the lavatory was the prettiest object he had ever seen in his life, a big diamond ring gleaming with blue-white radiance in the pre-dawn light.

If my theory were sound, Rascal had picked up the

ring and taken it to the back porch where Poe-the-Crow had spotted the treasure. This would explain the crow-raccoon fight which had awakened me.

Quite probably the black thief had won again—at least in the matter of flying away with the loot.

I had to ask permission of the kindly Reverend Hooton before starting my dusty climb to the seventy-five-foot belfry. The shaft was dark and filled with cobwebs and some of the cleats were loose, making me fear I might fall. But having enlisted in this venture, there could be no turning back. At long last I reached the airy little room at the top, with its widely spaced shutters, furnishing a view of the town and the creek winding toward the river. I stood for a few moments viewing the world below me. Then I touched the big deep-toned bell which had tolled forty-seven times for my mother and would one day toll ninety-nine times for my father.

Remembering my mission, I began to search the dusty belfry. Behind a pile of discarded hymnals which some dedicated idiot had lugged to this unlikely storage place I found the ragged circle of twigs and leaves and black feathers which Poe-the-Crow called home. As some people keep their money in their mattress, Poe had made his bed even more uncomfortable with a pile of shining junk which overran the nest and spilled across the floor. Here were glassies and steelies and one real agate marble, all of which he had stolen during our marble games. Here was my football whistle, snatched while he hovered just over the line of scrimmage shouting, "What fun! What fun!" Here were scraps of sheet copper, a second key to our Oldsmobile, and, wonder of wonders, Theo's diamond ring.

Poe dropped in at about this time, and he didn't say, "What fun!" He wouldn't let me pet him, and he cawed and swore at me as though *I* were the thief and *he* the honest householder.

I put several of these stolen articles into my pocket, my best marbles, the second key to our car, my football whistle, and Theo's ring, of course. But I left many of the shining trinkets, knowing that Poe couldn't tell sheet copper from a diamond ring. The crow's raucous criticism followed me all the way down that shaft and out into the sunlight.

Theo was so pleased at my recovery of her ring that she did not insist on the removal of my canoe from the living room. And she postponed the decision concerning a full-time housekeeper. She merely fed us delightful meals, and, with Jennie's help, left the house shining clean, with fresh curtains at the windows. Then with a good-by kiss and a wave of her hand she was off again— gallant and beautiful, brave and temperamental—and now no more.

III: *July*

Rascal had one virtue, rare in human beings, the capacity for gratitude. Feed him a favorite food, say a kind word, and he was your friend.

This simple approach to the heart of a raccoon produced some odd friendships in our neighborhood. Rascal's circle included Joe Hanks, the dim-witted janitor of the Methodist Church, who was convinced that the German Lutherans were planning to poison the water supply of Brailsford Junction.

"Stands to reason, don't it?" Joe said. "They got the water tower right up there on German Hill behind the Lutheran Church. All they got to do is drop a couple of little poison pills down the air vent and next morning we'll all wake up dead."

Joe was otherwise harmless. He pumped the pipe organ

when sober, and let me pump it when he started getting drunk. His secret for winning Rascal's affection came in his lunchbox. He always gave my raccoon half of one of his jelly sandwiches. Rascal thought Joe was one of the nicest people he had ever met.

Another friend was Bumblebee Jim Vandevander, the bald, three-hundred-pound son of our equally large washerwoman. Jim arrived every Monday morning pulling a little coaster wagon behind him to pick up our washing. and brought it back on Friday, clean, fresh-smelling, and beautifully ironed. On each arrival he gave Rascal a peppermint candy. What more could one ask of a friend?

Rascal couldn't, of course, read the calendar or the clock, but he knew almost to the minute when Bumblebee Jim was arriving and always became eager and talkative, anticipating his piece of candy. I finally concluded that raccoons, who do most of their hunting at night, have an extremely acute sense of hearing. Apparently Rascal was aware of the first faint rattle of the coaster wagon far off down the street.

From all the sounds of summer—the whirr of distant lawn mowers, the singing of the cicadas, the clip-clop of horses' hoofs, and the orchestration of the birds, Rascal could distinguish and identify, long before I could, the distant approach of the coaster wagon.

Not all of Rascal's motives were ulterior. He loved music for its own sake and had definite preferences among the records I played for him on the wind-up Victrola. Wagnerian sopranos hurt his ears. But he would sit, dreamy-eyed, listening to his favorite popular song: "There's a Long, Long Trail A-winding." In that ballad nightingales are mentioned.

I asked my father one morning if we have nightingales in America, or any other bird that sings at night.

"Not nightingales," he said, "but we do have whippoorwills, of course."

"I've never heard a whippoorwill."

"Can that be possible? Why, when I was a boy . . ." And he was off on a pilgrimage into the past when Wisconsin was still half wilderness, when panthers sometimes looked in through the windows, and the whippoorwills called all night long.

Thure Ludwig Theodor Kumlien (1819–88) always came into these reminiscences somewhere. He was a great pioneer naturalist, for whom the Kumlien gull, aster, and anemone were named. A contemporary of Thoreau and Audubon and Agassiz, he had been trained at Upsala in Sweden, and had come to southern Wisconsin in the 1840's, buying eighty acres adjoining the North homestead.

"Kumlien could start the whippoorwills any night by playing his flute," my father said. "Far across the fields we heard them, the old man with his flute, his son playing the violin, and hundreds of whippoorwills calling—that's music to remember."

It made me sad that I could not have known Kumlien, and walked the woods with him, learning every bird and flower and insect. I had been born too late, it seemed, even to hear a whippoorwill.

My father looked at me for a moment as though he were really seeing me.

"Let's take the day off," he said. "There must be a pair of whippoorwills somewhere around here."

Those were rare and gala days when my father took me rambling. While I slapped together a few cheese sandwiches, and packed half a dozen bottles of cold root beer and pop in the lunch basket, my father drove downtown to hang a sign on the office door:

Gone For The Day

He came back with the windshield down, the top back, and his white curls blowing in the wind. He was wearing a pair of motor goggles and looked very handsome and dashing, I thought. I put on my goggles too. Rascal, of course, wore his permanently. He perched between us on the back of the seat, gazing rapturously ahead.

We had sold the old Model T, and now were driving a huge seven-passenger Oldsmobile which my father had accepted in one of his numerous real estate swaps. It was rather large for the two of us, but we needed that big back seat for the occasions when we took Wowser with us. The Saint Bernard would never lie down in the car. He lumbered from one side to the other, peering forward with worried face and furrowed brow, occasionally woofing a deep-throated warning. But Wowser couldn't go today. He would frighten too many birds. The three of us were leaving him behind.

We were a happy trio as my father pulled down the

gas lever and roared from low into second, and from second into high. We took the Newville road which led toward Lake Koshkonong, one of the largest lakes in Wisconsin, which is formed by a widening in Rock River, and deepened by the dam at Indian Ford. In former years it had been covered in the shallows by hundreds of acres of wild rice which had attracted thousands of waterfowl and migrating bands of Indians. There were still many flocks of wild ducks and geese each spring and fall, and big pickerel and wall-eyed pike for which we sometimes trolled from a rowboat.

We swung upstream from Newville toward Taylor's point where an old resort hotel called the Lake House then stood. There were few cottages on Koshkonong in those days, merely groves and meadows, and miles of sand beaches. Several creeks entered shallow bays where great blue herons waded stealthily, striking as swiftly as a water snake to seize and swallow small fish and frogs.

We took the Lake House road, and followed a grassy lane to the limestone cliff jutting into the lake, a promontory crowned with white clover and shaded by magnificent old trees. My father set the emergency brake, and I chocked the wheels with large stones to be sure that the Oldsmobile would not bounce from that seventy-five-foot precipice into the lake.

Then all three of us went running out to the very tip of the point as though we were a little mad with happiness —as indeed we were. This was our very own lake, filling our life to the brim. We had each been born almost within the sound of its waves. Here we had spent our separate boyhoods. Here we fished and swam and canoed and searched for arrowheads.

The view from the point was superb. We could see the outlet of the lake into Rock River, downstream to our right, and ten miles away to our left the inlet in the blue haze.

My father's memories and mine differed, of course, for he had known these shores when they were heavily forested and he had visited the Indian wigwams on Crab Apple point, Thibault's point, and Charlie's bluff. At the age of twelve he had fallen slightly in love with a pretty Indian girl, so light-skinned and delicate of feature that my father was sure she was more than half French. The Indians had moved on, like the waterfowl they hunted, and with them went the girl, whom he never saw again.

Most prominent of all the points was a dark, lush projection which was the delta made by Koshkonong Creek —perhaps the wildest bit of woods and water in the entire region.

I had been careless in supervising Rascal, and I looked just in time to see him disappearing down a crooked ravine that angled through the limestone toward the lake. It was a moist and pleasant cleft in the rock with wild columbine blooming from every crevice, and it led by a devious and dangerous route to a little cave named for the Indian chief, Black Hawk. Rascal was only exploring, but I feared the small raccoon might take a dangerous tumble at the edge of the precipice.

"I'm going after him," I shouted to my father.

"Well, be careful, son," he said.

He was a casual parent who never tried to stop me from risking any hazard, even when I swam through the floodgates at Indian Ford. He knew I could climb like a squirrel and swim like an otter. So he had no worries about me now.

The little ravine, nicked into the cliff, was steep and slippery. But the chase was swift, for there, well ahead of me, was that ringed tail, disappearing around one turn after another.

"Come back here, Rascal," I shouted sternly. But the raccoon paid no attention. I pulled a sugar lump from my pocket, usually a successful recourse. But Rascal was having none of it. He did not hesitate a moment until he reached the sheer cliff with a twenty-foot drop to the cave's entrance, toward which he peered down eagerly.

I trilled in our mutual language and he responded. But over he went, scrambling backward down that wall of rock. I reached the edge a moment too late to stop him; and I could only hold my breath until he arrived safely at the cave.

There was nothing for it now but to inch my own way down that last twenty feet, catching a toe hold or finger hold wherever possible between the strata of limestone. In a few minutes, however, I too was safely at the entrance, which offered crawl space to the inner room.

It wasn't a large cave. But, by tradition, it had furnished Black Hawk a hiding place while he was being pursued by Abraham Lincoln, Jefferson Davis, and other young soldiers during the Black Hawk War. The episode was probably a myth, but the boys of that area who scrambled down to the small cavern believed every word of the story, and shuddered to think that the ghost of Black Hawk might be lurking there in the gloom.

The sandy floor of this cool hideaway was large enough for a small campfire and two or three campers. And there was a convenient ledge four feet above the floor, which furnished sleeping space for an uncomfortable night wrapped in blankets.

When my eyes grew accustomed to the dim light, I saw Rascal. He was prowling along the shelf of rock trying to reach the tiny, gleaming stalactites which hung from the low roof of the cave. He was reaching up with his eager little hands when I caught him.

I had no desire to punish him. I merely held him close. And Rascal told me in every way he could that I was completely forgiven for having cornered and captured him.

My father greeted us as we came safely up the cliff. He had been certain that I would rescue the raccoon, and then would survive the climb. Living much in the past. and never in the worrisome future, his outlook was so tranquil that he drifted pleasantly from 1862 to 1962— seven months short of a full century—with very little sense of personal or international tragedy. Curiously enough, this lifelong detachment accompanied an excellent university education, a vast store of disorganized knowledge, and a certain amount of charm.

"Whippoorwills," he explained, "are seldom seen in the daylight. They crouch on fence rails or the limbs of trees. If they flutter up for a moment they resemble giant Cecropia moths. We won't find them until after dusk, and that gives us many hours."

With the whole day ahead of us, we took our swimming trunks and the lunch basket and started down the long sloping path to the beach. My father was the acknowledged expert on the Indian trails of southern Wisconsin.

"This was a Fox-Winnebago-Sac trail," my father said. "It was used by Black Hawk and his warriors and by their pursuers. These large burial mounds were probably made by much earlier tribes."

Along these trails were to be found bird-points, hunting arrows, skinning knives, and scrapers, mostly of flint. In my father's fine collection there were also black and gleaming obsidian spear points, some of them eight inches long, red calumets transported from Minnesota, and copper ornaments from the Lake Superior region.

As we progressed downward toward the beach, Rascal trundled along obediently, panting in the manner of dogs and raccoons when they are hot. The sight of glistening water ahead, cool and inviting, increased his gait to a gallop.

I paused to examine his tracks which made a design like beadwork on an Indian quiver. The handprints and footprints resembled those of a very small human baby. Where Rascal had been *walking*, the imprint of the retreating left hand was paired with that of the advancing right foot, and vice versa. But where he had broken into a *gallop*, all four tracks tended to bunch.

For all his intelligent adaptability, my small friend was aided in every act by intricate and inborn patterns of raccoon behavior.

On this curve of the shore a very cold, spring-fed rivulet rushed down from the hills, twisting among glacial boulders and the roots of oak trees to fan across the white sand to the lake. In a pool of this stream I placed the bottles of root beer and pop, awaiting our picnic.

My father and I donned swimming trunks, and soon all three of us were in the lake. Sandpipers tipped and scurried along the beach, darting in and out as the waves advanced or retreated. Rails slithered through the reeds, and somewhere, safely hidden, an American bittern began to "pump" his odd, deep note, like the sound of a sledge hammer driving a fencepost into marshy soil.

My father was a strong swimmer, using the old-fashioned breast stroke. I was very proud of the fact that I had learned the fast, effective Australian crawl. But Rascal could only dog-paddle.

He came along bravely, however, keeping his nose out of water, indicating again that raccoons probably can't dive. For a three-month-old he was doing excellently. But soon he was panting from the exertion and looking to me as his natural protector. We were in deep water now, and the best I could do for him was to roll over on my back in a floating position, arch my chest, and offer him a good platform. He scrambled gratefully aboard, whimpering slightly in self-pity. But soon he had regained his courage and his breath, and in he plunged again.

I had thought that Rascal had demonstrated his top speed, but as we came around a grassy point I learned my error. There, to her surprise and ours, was the modest mate of the glamorous mallard drake—garbed in becoming brown, and leading a late nesting of downy ducklings. This mallard mother had eleven beautiful babies, light as thistledown, following her for dear life in a straight-line flotilla.

Rascal accelerated by at least ten percent upon seeing the tempting sight ahead. He obviously had visions of a juicy duckling dinner. I wanted to forestall this slaughter, but my father said quietly, "Wait a minute, son, and watch what happens."

The ducklings performed a marvelous maneuver around the mother duck while she turned back to face the intruder. Putting herself between her endangered brood and Rascal, she swam directly toward the raccoon with no more fear than as though he had been a musk-rat. On came my crazy pet. On came the determined mother duck. It seemed a duel to the death, or at least a head-on collision.

At the last possible moment the mallard used her wings and was partially airborne. She aimed one strong and accurate blow of her bill between Rascal's avid eyes, flew over his head, and wheeled to join her ducklings.

Rascal wasn't actually hurt, but his pride was wounded. He swam back to me talking about it sorrowfully, and I gave him another rest after his shattering experience. In a few minutes he began to pretend he had forgotten all about that duckling dinner; and soon we went ashore for other food.

Raccoons have a passion for turtle eggs, and search for them on every beach. The turtles bury their eggs in the sand to let them be hatched by the warmth of the sun. But many a nest of eggs becomes a banquet for a raccoon.

Rascal had never been told about turtle eggs. But his keen nostrils informed him that somewhere in this sand was a gastronomic delight he had never sampled.

For at least three seconds he froze in the manner of a bird dog coming to a point. Then he began digging more furiously than he had ever dug before. Success! Up they came, all thirty-four of them, almost as big as golf balls, meaning that they were the eggs of a big snapping turtle. For the next half hour Rascal was with us physically, but elsewhere in spirit, obviously in some realm where gourmet raccoons feast for eternity, their eyes on the stars while their swift hands and sharp little teeth tear open turtle eggs to gorge upon them.

While we ate our picnic lunch, Rascal was busy slightly depleting the next generation of snapping turtles. He was so completely satiated that he even refused the last few sips of my strawberry pop.

The sun was past the meridian, but there were many summer hours to squander before we might hear the first evening whippoorwill.

My father, who owned farms in this region, decided we

might as well visit them to see how the tobacco was leafing out, and how the wheat harvest was progressing.

It should be said in passing that "ownership" of a piece of property was never that simple with my father. Although he never touched a card, he was a born gambler particularly in real estate. When he took title to a farm he immediately loaded it with a first mortgage and usually a second mortgage. With the money thus liberated he would buy another farm and repeat the process. It was very much like buying securities on a margin. When the market was rising, he pyramided his paper profits. But in every farm recession he came close to disaster.

I didn't understand his complex bookkeeping, and perhaps he didn't either. But at this moment he felt he was fairly wealthy, with a wheat ranch in Montana, and some eight or ten other pieces of endangered property.

My mother hadn't lived to see much of this new prosperity. A delicate, highly intelligent woman, she had entered college at the age of fourteen and graduated at the head of her class. She had accepted and married my father, for better or for worse, sharing more years of poverty than of comfort. She did the worrying for the family; and it was largely worry that killed her at forty-seven. My father, who lived in an insulated dream world, took all of his losses philosophically, even the loss of my mother.

On this summer day in 1918 he had no worries whatsoever, unless he briefly remembered that Herschel was fighting in the front lines in France. The price of leaf tobacco was soaring as were the prices of other farm products, and land was selling at an all-time high. His corn fields were green and thriving and his wheat and oats were promising a record yield to the acre. In lush pastures through which small brooks wandered, his herds of Holstein and Guernsey cattle grazed contentedly in knee-deep grass and clover.

I always enjoyed these farm excursions, particularly the opportunity to watch colts and calves high-tailing through the pastures. The young of almost every species, it seemed, were glad to be alive, Rascal included.

Just now, however, my little raccoon was happily exhausted, sleeping off his overindulgence in turtle eggs. He lay on the back seat, his ringed tail coiled neatly over his face. He continued to sleep until "first lamp light" when we were nearing our destination in search of whippoorwills.

We had no time to visit the site of the cabin where my father had been born or the big brick house on the same homestead where he had spent his boyhood. If we were to reach the Kumlien property, we must leave the car at this point and walk through meadowland along the old Milwaukee trail, long since abandoned. Up this trail from Galena, Illinois had once moved heavy oxcarts pulled by six or eight yoke of oxen. These "toad-crushers," bringing pigs of lead from the mines to the lake port, had wheels made of the cross sections of giant white oak trees. The screaming of these wheels on their wooden axles could be heard for miles.

Down this same trail from Milwaukee had come such early settlers as Thure Kumlien from Sweden and my ancestors from England.

The ruts were now overgrown with grass, and healed by the passage of time, but we could see them clearly as my father, Rascal, and I walked through the gathering dusk accompanied only by the shadows of pioneers long dead, moving through fields and forests of memory.

Above us circled the nighthawks searching insects, their aerial acrobatics graceful and erratic.

"Notice the ovals of white under each wing," my father said. "That is one of the few ways you can tell nighthawks from whippoorwills."

"What other ways?"

"The whippoorwill's call, of course, and his whiskers."

"How can you get near enough to see a whippoorwill's whiskers?"

"You seldom can," my father admitted, "but on those which Kumlien mounted, they were obvious enough: stiff bristles on either side of the wide mouth, probably for sensing the flying insects he scoops up for food."

We walked on in silence approaching the forty acres of virgin forest which Kumlien had protected from the ax. It is gone now, but it was there when I was a boy, a sanctuary and a memorial, haunted by the spirit of the gentle Swede who played his flute for the whippoorwills.

We came at last to the flowing well which the old naturalist had dug, ringed with heavy limestone slabs, its cold water gushing up from below and winding off in a little stream through marshy pastures to the lake.

I was thirsty and went down on my knees to drink from the clear deep pool. But my father said, "Wait a minute, Sterling. Try this."

From mint that Kumlien had once planted my father plucked a few leaves, asked me to rub them between my fingers and then taste them thoroughly. They were delightful and tangy. And when I drank from the well, I tasted water more cool and refreshing than any I had ever known. In the amber afterlight around that woodland spring we all three drank; then amid the ferns we waited for my first whippoorwill.

Very slowly the full moon edged above the horizon until we could see its entire circumference. Rascal roamed a bit, and caught and ate a cricket. But he was still too well fed to be restless. He came back to me, chirring comfortably, and to his chirr were added other night sounds, the wings of big moths soft upon the air, the rustling of small creatures in the grass, meadow mice perhaps, and the chorus of the frogs in the marsh.

Then, then it came! Three pure syllables, three times repeated:

Whip-poor-will, whip-poor-will, whip-poor-will.

A soloist against the symphony of the night making me feel weightless, airborne, and eerie—happy, but also immeasurably sad.

Again the whippoorwill called. And on this second invitation another whippoorwill answered courteously. For nearly half an hour they carried on their spirited duet.

My small raccoon sat listening intently, well aware of the exact direction from which each call was coming. Having had his afternoon nap, he was now ready to make a night of it.

The concert ended as abruptly as it had begun, and we awoke as from a dream. We scrambled up from the ferns, and by the light of the rising moon, turned westward down the old trail which had brought my people to this land of lakes and rivers.

IV: *August*

THE heavy fighting around Soissons in July 1918 shocked Brailsford Junction out of its complacency. As the casualty lists grew, and personal tragedy came to one home after another, we seemed much nearer to the trenches and the shell-shattered wheat fields of France, red with poppies and with blood.

One of the first reactions of the saddened town was to forbid the war games we had been playing each Saturday on Earl's Hill. It seemed a shame, after all our work constructing dugouts and opposing trench systems; for we had thoroughly enjoyed our desperate battles. The only participant to protest loudly was Slammy Stillman, the overgrown town bully, who never had played fair. He was the only boy who threw stones instead of the regulation clods of earth, and the only one who sometimes aimed at our Red Cross nurses who were identified by the dish towel each girl draped over her head.

The ceremony that really drove home the grim fact that war is not a game was the service held in memory of Rollie Adams, one of the most-admired boys in town. Neighbors of all faiths came to the Methodist Church to hear Reverend Hooton remind us that Rollie had never hurt or hated anyone. The big service flag had been taken down and placed across the lap of Rollie's mother. Her part of the ceremony was to remove a service star and to sew on the gold one. Everyone wept, and the war seemed terribly near. I found myself praying silently that Herschel's star would not be changed to gold. We wouldn't even have had Mother there to sew it on.

There was a flurry of patriotism among the children of the town, the girls knitting khaki wristlets by the score, and the boys competing to see who could collect the most peach pits, used in making charcoal for gas masks.

Another lively contest was the scramble for tin foil. Up and down the streets and alleys went the tin-foil hunters, each child for himself. But I had a helper. As soon as Rascal dimly perceived the general idea, he ranged ahead of me searching the gutters for the shining foil. My ball of foil was one of the largest, thanks to an occasional contribution made by my raccoon.

Rascal's only other assistance in the war effort was the help he gave me in my garden. While I hoed, he trundled along behind me like a little dog. He also helped me pick peas from a late planting. All the peas he picked, however, he kept for himself, opening each pod as though it were a small clam, and avidly shelling the green pearls into his mouth. He had little relish for the wax beans which were coming on by the bushel; so, while I picked beans, he often took a comfortable siesta in the shade of the rhubarb leaves.

It was pleasant out there in my garden, warmed by the sun, cooled by an occasional breeze. The wax beans were golden and smooth, with the texture of satin, and they hung in such thick clusters beneath their leaves that it did not take long to fill a basket. Although the grocery stores paid me well for my vegetables, it was reward enough just to plant and harvest such a garden. My mother had told me that seeds carry in their "memory" the whole complex pattern of stem and leaf and flower and fruit, and she had shown me how the stamens and pistils begin the seed-making process all over again. It seemed miraculous then, and no less miraculous now.

I had been noticing that my little raccoon also carried patterns in his brain, as do the migrating birds and the honey-storing bees. I think I learned more about the orderly universe sitting in my garden picking beans than I ever did on a hard church pew listening to Reverend Hooton's sermons.

One serious mistake I made, however, was to give Rascal his first taste of sweet corn. I twisted a plump ear from a stalk in one of my rows, stripped back the husk, and handed the corn to my pet, who had carefully watched the whole performance. Rascal went slightly berserk. No other food he had ever tasted compared to this juicy new delicacy which he was sampling for the

73

first time. He ate most of the first ear, then in a frenzy scrambled up another corn stalk, pulling it slowly to the ground. He wrestled and struggled with a fresh ear, tearing away part of the husk and guzzling greedily as before. Still unsatisfied, he left the second ear half eaten to climb a third corn stalk. He was drunk and disorderly on the nectar and ambrosia called sweet corn.

I thought Rascal's binge was amusing. But when I told the story to my father, he looked at us both quite seriously and said, "I'm afraid you're in for trouble, Sterling."

I certainly was in for trouble. Rascal spent less than half the ensuing night in our bed—which didn't disturb me too greatly, since sleeping with a raccoon in August is a little too warm for comfort. I was aware that he must have let himself out, and gone on a neighborhood prowl. But this was not unusual.

On subsequent nights he took similar French leave. And he began sleeping soundly through most of the daylight hours.

I didn't connect his nocturnal ramblings with his love for sweet corn, principally because he avoided our corn patch. The explanation was simple. To keep my woodchucks out of our garden we had surrounded it with a woven-wire fence and installed a gate with a strong latch. Rascal could have climbed that fence, but found it more convenient to raid the gardens of our neighbors.

August is an intemperate month in any case when emotions go up with the thermometer. But the angry voices to be heard on our street each morning were sizzling even for August. One neighbor after another—easygoing, salty Mike Conway, handsome, slightly vain Walter Dabbett, the skinflint lumber dealer Cy Jenkins, and the terrible-tempered Reverend Thurman—found their respective sweet-corn patches mauled by some fiendish night raider. Plans for detection and revenge were under way.

It was Cy Jenkins who found raccoon tracks in the dust between his corn rows and spread the news.

My father was right. I was facing *real* trouble. A delegation arrived one evening to sit in a circle around my unfinished canoe, voicing their complaints while Rascal huddled in my lap for protection.

"I seen that varmint's tracks right in my garden," Jenkins said triumphantly.

"Like the seven plagues of Egypt," Thurman sermonized.

"Now, Sterling, we like your little raccoon," Mrs. Dabbett began.

"But the next time he gets in my sweet corn . . . ," her husband warned.

The threats came whizzing around us like the buzz of angry hornets.

"Next moonlight night I'll shoot him."

"I'll set a trap, so help me."

"Skunks, woodchucks, 'coons! What next?"

"Now, just a moment," my father said quietly. (Among other civic responsibilities, he served as justice of the peace, and knew from long experience how to handle a group of angry people.)

Mike Conway was willing to listen. "What do you suggest?"

"If Sterling buys a collar and leash for his raccoon . . ."

"Not enough," Cy Jenkins growled.

"And builds him a cage . . . ," my father added.

Rascal began to whimper, and I looked anxiously from face to face. Most were grim, but Mrs. Dabbett gave me a sympathetic glance, before turning to glare at her husband.

Reverend Thurman, belonging to a sect which will here remain nameless, glowered at my father and thundered. "Vengeance is mine, saith the Lord." Thurman had been under his Model T all day using pulpit words but not in the Sunday manner. Something about his inappropriate quotation from Holy Writ struck Mike Conway as funny. Mike had a lusty and infectious laugh. And when he threw back his head and roared, everyone except Thurman joined in the chorus.

"Well, it's settled then," my father said. "Sterling, why don't you bring some glasses and a pitcher of cold grape juice?"

Thurman and Jenkins didn't stay for the refreshments. But the rest of us enjoyed the cool drink, Rascal taking his from a saucer.

"I'm sorry," Mrs. Dabbett said to me as she was leaving. "Rascal didn't know he was doing wrong."

After the neighbors were gone I said bitterly to my father, "You can put criminals in jail. But you can't put my good little raccoon in jail. How would you like to be led around on a leash?"

76

"Now, Sterling," my father said soothingly, "it's better than having Rascal shot or trapped."

"Well, all right. But I think Rascal and I will run away and live in a cabin in the woods somewhere."

"In the woods?"

"As far from people as we can get—way up in the north woods on the shore of Lake Superior, maybe."

My father pondered this for a moment and then said, "How would you like to take a two-week trip, all the way to Superior? Bring Rascal along of course!"

"Do you really mean it?"

"Of course I mean it. You can ask the Conway boys to feed Wowser and take care of your war garden."

I snatched Rascal from the rug and started dancing crazily, which didn't disturb my raccoon. He was always ready for a romp. We had been given a reprieve—a wonderful two-week reprieve.

"When can we start, Daddy?"

"Why, tomorrow I suppose," my father said. "I'll just put a sign on the office door."

There were no superhighways in those days to streak impersonally toward some distant goal, scoring the countryside with ribbons of unfeeling concrete. In fact there was scant paving of any kind, only friendly little roads that wandered everywhere, muddy in wet weather, dusty in dry, but clinging to ancient game and Indian trails, skirting orchards where one might reach out to pluck an early apple, winding through the valleys of streams and rivers, coming so close to flower gardens and pastures of clover that one could smell all the good country smells, from new-mown hay to ripening corn.

We started early the next morning, my father, Rascal, and I in our usual places on the front seat. Turning northward toward Fort Atkinson, we passed our old farm and the Kumlien place as we ascended the Rock River valley. Finding the sources of streams was a passion with me. I had followed Saunder's Creek all the way to its first spring nearly ten miles north of Brailsford Junction, and I had always wanted to follow the Rock River to its source. So we went by way of the Horicon marshes, as romantic to me as Sidney Lanier's Marshes of Glynn.

At some point in this neighborhood we crossed the divide between waters pouring down the Rock River to the Mississippi and waters pouring into Lake Winnebago and the Fox River to Lake Michigan, and thus down the Lakes to the St. Lawrence and the Atlantic. When we saw the first creek running northeastward I felt like the early French explorers of this region.

We skirted Lake Winnebago for many miles, from Fond du Lac to Neenah and Menasha where Winnebago empties into the Fox, there to cascade in several major rapids on its winding journey to Green Bay.

We were making excellent time, considering the bumpy roads and two blowouts, which in those days one took with serenity, struggling with tire irons, inner tubes likely to be pinched, and hand pumps to inflate the tires.

We had packed some of my casual sandwiches, hard-boiled eggs, fresh peaches, and a dozen doughnuts. There was no reason to bring any special food for Rascal. He ate almost anything, just as though he were a person—which he definitely believed he was. We bought a tin pail of fresh, cold milk at a farmhouse and feasted beside a bridge over a rushing stream. When Rascal had eaten, he curled up on the cushion of the big back seat—a coil of shining fur against the maroon leather. And there he slept happily all the afternoon.

It is even more exciting to move from one arboreal region into another than to move from watershed to watershed. This second "divide" we were crossing was from the deciduous trees of southern Wisconsin—the elms, maples, oaks, and hickories—into the evergreen region of pines, spruce, hemlock, and cedars.

Now the farm odors and fragrances blended into the great perfume of the north woods: the sharp spicy aroma of the firs, and the fine hot scent of the pine needles lying four inches thick to blanket the forest floor.

We began to see the first granite and basalt rock formations of the oldest geologic period of the world, the Canadian Shield which carries in its treasure house some of the richest ores on the continent—iron, copper, silver, and many other minerals.

My father knew enough geology and minerology to show me where the salts of copper had stained a cliff blue with azurite and green with malachite. These colors blended with assurance into the moss and lichen on the rocks, adding their tints to those of sky and water.

I felt a twinge of conscience to be so carried away with this new and different beauty of northern Wisconsin. It was as though I were being unfaithful to southern Wisconsin and to my own lake—Koshkonong.

In those days there were no motels, and few other places to sleep along the highway, unless in a tent or under the open sky. I wanted to be a *voyageur* on this excursion, sleeping without cover. My father was willing to gamble against rain, being as little concerned as I.

We stopped on a point which extended into a small clear lake, unpacked such duffel as we needed, and arranged our camp. Safely out on an extremity of bare granite, its crystals possibly two billion years old, we built a modest fire to cook our evening meal.

I went to the bottom of the cliff, with rod and reel, to cast a wet fly toward an inviting expanse of ivory-white water lilies. On my fifth cast an eager black bass—two and one-half pounds perhaps—seized the lure and tangled himself in the lilies. I brought him out at last, eyes lustrous, scales shining.

Cleaned, filleted, and fried golden brown, he made an appetizing fish course for three hungry campers there among the pines.

We had no tent—only navy hammocks. Still trusting this bright, clear August weather, fringed everywhere with goldenrod and asters, we consigned ourselves to the canopy of the sky.

That first night we tied one end of each hammock to spruce trees, the other to the rear bumper of the Oldsmobile. We had our easily imaginable difficulties climbing aboard these tipsy platforms of canvas while also pulling the blankets around us.

My father said he would show me how it was done. Firmly grasping the dowel pin which spread the upper end of the canvas, he eased himself onto his treacherous bed. But before he could cover himself with a blanket the hammock flipped upside down. He landed unhurt but exasperated on the thick padding of spruce and pine needles.

I laughed until I was breathless, and Rascal hurried over to see why my father was lying on the ground muttering to himself.

"I'll bet it's easy," I said confidently. I made a running dive, lit squarely in the hammock, held it for a minute, and then did a somersault.

Now my father was laughing as hard as I was, and Rascal was scampering around as though he understood the joke. Just then, at the most appropriate moment, something *else* began to laugh—maniacal, spine-chilling laughter from far across the lake.

"Holy Moses, what's that?"

"That's a loon," my father said, "and he's laughing at *us*—he thinks we're crazy trying to sleep in navy hammocks."

I was suddenly completely happy, in love with the loony world and with my father and Rascal. I didn't care where I slept, or how many times I tipped out of my hammock.

The new moon came up—a sliver of silver through the pointed firs on the far edge of the lake. And the fragrance of balsam and pine swept over the darkening point.

We learned at last how to sleep in a hammock and

still cover ourselves with our blankets. Soon we dropped into blissful slumber with Rascal beside me. Little screech owls sang our lullaby, and at the base of the cliff there was a gentle swish-swish of small waves—the most soothing sound in the world.

It was shortly after midnight that the brakes began to slip. The first warning came when we bumped the ground gently in our collapsing hammocks. The car was backing slowly toward us. My father, thinking fast, threw a stone under a rear wheel. Rascal awoke more swiftly than I did and went prowling around the car as though he thought we were being attacked.

My father and I were so sleepy that we merely removed the more obvious sticks and stones, rearranged the pine needles under our hammocks, and went back to sleep again. That was the way we would fix our beds from this night on—flat on the ground, the only way you can possibly sleep in a hammock.

After a few growls and whimpers and trills, Rascal came back to crawl in with me under my warm blankets.

The cool night went on without us, oblivious of this small intrusion of humanity. And the gentle serenade continued—a night heron's distant croak, the footfall of a fox, fish splashing in the pale moonlight. The sidereal universe went wheeling around us, pivoted on the North Star—which, as a very small child, I thought was named for *us* when Mother first had shown me the Great Dipper and the star toward which it points.

We awoke at dawn, wonderfully refreshed by a night in the pine-scented air. My father said he felt a little stiff. But I challenged him to join us for a swim in the icy lake. We dipped, toweled dry, and raced up the path to the cliff, panting and laughing, with Rascal dripping gaily along behind. For breakfast we had bacon sandwiches and the remaining peaches, with black coffee from a graniteware pot.

As we sat munching our sandwiches, utterly contented, a very large bird came soaring over the lake. I spotted him first.

"Look, a bald eagle!"

My father watched the bird for several moments before he said, "No, son, but you were close. It's an osprey."

"How can you tell?"

"An eagle soars on straight pinions. The osprey has a slight bend in the wings. Our bird is only crested with white. The mature bald eagle has a head which is entirely white."

Obviously there was much I still could learn from my father, who explained complicated matters so simply.

Rascal was begging for the last of my sandwich, standing on his capable hind legs, patting my cheek and reaching for the food. So I lay on the ground at his level and we looked each other squarely in the eye as we nibbled at either end of the bacon sandwich, growling softly, just for the joy of pretending we were fighting a little over the food we were sharing.

Soon we were packed, and off into the morning through

pine shadows and patches of sunlight which dappled a winding road through the forest.

One of the several poems which I knew by heart at this age was Keats' "On First Looking into Chapman's Homer":

> Then felt I like some watcher of the skies
> When a new planet swims into his ken;
> Or like stout Cortez when with eagle eyes
> He star'd at the Pacific—and all his men
> Look'd at each other with a wild surmise—
> Silent, upon a peak in Darien.

My sister Jessica, the poet of our family, had told me that it was probably Balboa, and certainly not Cortez, who had caught this particular glimpse of the Pacific. Her criticism did not lessen my admiration for the sonnet, however. I was still in that uncritical stage which allows for the enjoyment of poetry.

We came upon Lake Superior with similar astonishment and wild surmise—an entire ocean stretching far beyond the horizon, as though a sapphire half as big as the visible sky had been set among granite cliffs and northern pines.

This "sea of sweet water," as Radisson had called it when he had visited these shores in the autumn of 1659, is the largest and deepest of the Great Lakes. No cleaner, colder, or more crystal water will be found upon our continent. It is rightly named Superior, having no equal in the world.

From our eminence above Chequamegon Bay we could see several of the Apostle Islands blending into the far distance. As we hurried toward the lake I found myself reluctantly admitting that this tremendous bowl of blue water was indeed more beautiful than my Koshkonong.

On a shore of sparkling sand and clean-washed gravel, with the gulls crying overhead, my father and Rascal and I walked the beach, like beachcombers in a dream. This might have been Crusoe's island, we were so alone with sea and sky.

In a little pool made by an entering rivulet, my raccoon caught a gleaming minnow which proved to be a trout—dappled with color. Rascal next explored the whitened stumps washed up by the waves. Through these labyrinths he felt his way, curious but cautious, apparently expecting to meet the rightful owner at any moment.

The beaches of Lake Superior are strewn with agates. These ancient jewels are the result of age-long water seepage into small cavities in the rock. The water carries silica in solution, stained by various minerals. The result is often a gem which in cross section shows rings within rings of crocus yellow through all the shades of brown to deep, rich red. On the outside, agates are often pitted and with no visible evidence of their interior beauty— which rivals the most subtle stained glass. If by accident broken open, however, they shine, wet and radiant upon the beach. During that morning we found more than twenty stones worthy of cutting and polishing.

Rascal knew nothing about agates, picking up and dropping almost any bright stone that took his eye. But he did find one of the broken agates; and I kept it for him to add to his pennies and his arrowhead. In time he grew impatient with this beach which seemed to have no crayfish, and went to sleep in the hollow of an old stump until we also tired of the agate hunt.

We ate at a small restaurant in Ashland, then followed the road westward which brought us into the valley of the Brule River, the finest trout stream in Wisconsin.

Needing supplies, we stopped at an old, unpainted crossroads store. There was everything imaginable for sale in that store: snowshoes, shotguns and deer rifles, and even a yoke for oxen. You could buy groceries as well as brightly colored yard goods, snow packs, and bear traps. There was also merchandise more fascinating to me, such as excellent split-bamboo fly rods and hand-tied trout flies which I viewed with longing.

While my father bought bread, bacon, and other necessities, Rascal and I browsed. I had been taught never to touch things when I shopped, but Rascal had no such scruples. He delicately fingered everything shiny at his level—never cutting himself or tipping over the object. His little hands examined gleaming axes, peavey hooks, and entrancing fly reels. On and on went his happy investigation of log chains, garden tools, and other hardware. Only when he climbed on a counter and started touching the kerosene lamps did I stop him for fear he might send one crashing to the floor.

"Real smart 'coon you got there," the storekeeper said. "Make a good coonskin cap some day."

"He'll never be a coonskin cap," I said fiercely, and

surprised at the anger in my voice. "Nobody will ever skin Rascal."

We came at last to what was to be our permanent camp in the north woods. It was on a promontory some twenty feet above one of the deepest and most beautiful trout pools I have ever seen, carved from the rock at a curve in the Brule. The grove shading the little hill was the only piece of virgin timber we found in all that north country. If the trees had been *white* pine they would have been cut forty years previously. But they were *yellow* pine—just as proud in the forest, but almost useless to the carpenter, who calls this intractable wood "Devil pine" because it cracks and splinters in every direction and refuses to take a nail without a tantrum.

The nearest branches were at least thirty-five feet above us, and the forest floor beneath had no vegetation, only a thick carpet of pine needles. The breeze was always gently stirring in this high-canopied room, and again we had a projecting rock above the river for safe campfires. When the sun sank slowly westward through our pine-roofed mansion, we ate, and prepared our beds upon the ground. I had almost decided that I would live here forever, thus avoiding permanently the nightmare of caging my pet raccoon.

It was characteristic of my parent that he had not told me the real reason for this trip. He had been asked to testify as an expert witness in a case being tried before a judge in Superior, Wisconsin.

Our camp on the Brule was some twenty miles from the courtroom; so each day the court was in session, my father would leave shortly after breakfast, taking his packet of notes and documents, and would return during the afternoon.

I had no interest in legal affairs, and my father was tranquil concerning my safety. He knew that I could scarcely get lost if I stayed on the river or one of its branches, and that Rascal and I could swim if we fell into one of the deeper pools. Several recent showers lessened the danger of forest fires, and we had seen no sign of bears—neither footprints along the stream nor trees scratched or rubbed at bear's length above the ground.

Despite the war in Europe, the world as a whole seemed safe in those days. We had left our house unlocked in Brailsford Junction. We seldom took the key from the car. We trusted our fellow human beings, and particularly the creatures of the woods.

Two weeks of absolute freedom! Each hour was savored. The very first day Rascal and I found an opening in the forest where a sunny hillside was festooned with blueberries nearly as large and dark as grapes, their leaves lacquered deep red. We hurried back to camp for a bucket, and returned to pick three or four quarts of such delicious fruit that I ate a third as many as I put in the pail. Rascal had an even better record. He ate every blueberry he picked.

That afternoon we were too busy exploring to find time to fish. Wearing only my swimming trunks, I padded over pine needles, as alluring to my bare feet as to Rascal's.

We crossed small tributaries to the Brule, or waded up their winding shallows hoping to find the hidden springs from which they emerged. We walked the length of mossy logs, crossed and recrossed the Brule in its foaming riffles—ice cold and amber clear. Once I slipped on a submerged boulder and went laughing down into the pool below, with Rascal plunging in dutifully to follow me in my fun. Little red pine squirrels scolded us as though we had interrupted a service in a cathedral. Striped chipmunks came darting out, whistling and chirping, frantic with curiosity and eager to see the show.

We had wandered far up the stream, and now the sun told us we should be getting back to camp. A pleasant breeze was tempering the August heat as we retraced our path—sometimes in and sometimes out of water. Rascal fished the river's edge feasting on minnows. I was seeing enough big trout where the sun struck deep into the pools to know that here was a stream to rival Isaak Walton's River Dove.

When we arrived at camp we were astonished to find a robber in the process of gnawing his way into the wooden box which contained our salt, flour, and other dry groceries. I had never before seen a porcupine, although my father had told me about them, and this could be none other than the very animal—clumsy, pug-nosed, and bristling with quills. Porcupines can't throw their quills. These barbed harpoons, however, leave the original owner at a touch, but stay in the flesh of his enemies like fishhooks.

Rascal had raced ahead for a closer look, but suddenly

grew cautious. All of his ancestors seemed to be whispering in his ear—"Careful! It's a porcupine!"

I didn't want to kill the intruder. Using a long stick, I nudged him gently toward a small tree up which he scrambled until he looked like a hawk's nest in the highest crotch. Then I went to examine the damage to our stores. It was our salt he had craved. He had ripped the salt box wide open and eaten enough to make him thirsty for the next six months. He wouldn't stay up that tree very long, I concluded. He would have to come down and go to the river for a drink.

Rascal and I lay on our backs drinking cold pop from a case we kept in a nearby spring.

"I'll bet he wishes he had a bottle of pop," I said to Rascal, as we gazed up at the thirsty porcupine. But Rascal was too busy to pay much attention.

Holding his bottle with both hands and both feet he drank as fast as a little raccoon can. He had no intimation that this free life would not go on forever or that he would soon be headed homeward to captivity.

One loses sense of time in the woods. I had no watch to replace my broken Ingersoll and could only guess at the hour of the day by looking at the sun. I had even forgotten what day it was—and it certainly didn't matter. No schoolbell or churchbell rang to remind us of the dutiful passage of time. One day blended into the next and could only be remembered as the day we saw the porcupine or the day we found Lost Lake.

It may have been the second or third day that Rascal

and I followed one of the larger upstream branches of the Brule far into the woods in search of its source. I had brought my fishpole, a can of worms, and a creel, but I wasn't having much luck with trout, only two eight-inchers which I unhooked carefully and returned unharmed to the stream. Brook trout are almost too beautiful to keep, being, in these waters, dark above with rosettes of filtered sunlight along their sides, some as red as wintergreen berries and some almost golden. They are amber pale beneath—part of the water itself, and of the spirit of the woods.

As usual the pine squirrels scolded; and once a ruffed grouse burst from cover with an explosion of wing music, burrowing off through the slanting sunlight of the forest. Rascal turned to me for protection and asked his usual questions. I assured him there was no danger, and laughed at him for being afraid of a grouse. Somewhere in the neighborhood there were grouse chicks hiding, all but invisible in the pine needles and old leaves. I didn't want Rascal to find them, so I told him to come along. On we went, up and up that rushing woodland stream.

It seemed a miracle that anything as young as fingerling trout or grouse chicks or my small raccoon could move along this watercourse among boulders as old as the world—the new life of this very season amid granite predating even the first life on the globe.

My mother, before she died, had revealed a few simple facts about the earliest forms of life on earth, and had tried to explain the story of creation in the Bible as a means by which a primitive and poetic people sought to record the beginning of things.

This does not mean there is no God, she said, or that He didn't create heaven and earth, darkness and light, and the seas and the land—yes, and millions of suns and planets, whole galaxies of distant stars. His spirit does move upon the face of the waters.

Then patiently, like the very good teacher she was, my mother had explained in words I could understand how the plants and animals had evolved from the simpler forms of life to the wonderfully complex flora and fauna of our present era. And I had thought there was no one more gracious or knowing than my mother, and nothing more pleasant than the sound of her voice. She seemed very close to me now as Rascal and I made our way up this branch of the Brule.

The stream came winding toward us over and under mossy logs. It tumbled through the remains of an abandoned beaver dam, and ran like quicksilver across the beaver meadow where meadow larks added their music to that of the water.

Then, half a mile farther upstream, we came upon it suddenly—a little lake which was the very source, as round as a big drop of dew and as clear. Its shores were of clean sand and gravel, and it was cupped among low hills, forested with evergreens, with several white birches standing in sharp relief against this background of dark firs.

There were water lilies in the shallows, their floating pads large enough for little frogs to sit on, and blossoms the size of saucers, where green and scarlet dragonflies held court.

We had come so quietly over the pine needles that the bathers had not seen us, and they were withers-deep in the lake—the first white-tail doe and the first fawn I had ever gazed upon, except in nature books. Then Rascal saw them, and was smitten by one of his crazy ideas. He slipped into the water and took the shortest route toward the deer, creating no more disturbance than an otter, and causing the doe and fawn no concern. The fawn and little raccoon had almost touched noses when the doe sensed me, blew a note of warning to her fawn, and lunged from the lake, calling to her offspring to follow. For a moment she hesitated and looked back toward me with great liquid eyes. Then doe and fawn went bounding off through the willows, throwing their white flags into the sunlight.

Rascal came paddling back very pleased with himself —thinking he had performed a brave service by frightening these intruders from a lake which now was ours by right of discovery and conquest.

On another day Rascal and I turned downstream on a fishing expedition. Because I did not own a fly rod, and had never had an opportunity to master the difficult and delicate art of manipulating a dry fly, I substituted the next best lure, a wet fly which I cast as one does a bass plug, retrieving this streamer in short jerks as though it were a wounded minnow.

In a likely pool half a mile downstream I felt a powerful lunge as a hungry trout struck that old bucktail. But the fish had missed the hook, and refused to strike again. More than ever I yearned for a fly rod and an assortment of dry flies to fish these trout as they should be fished.

Rascal was having better luck than I. He examined the river's edge with contemplative fingers, turning over small rocks in search of crayfish. The past and future meant nothing to Rascal; he lived completely in the present without ambition or worry, a very comfortable fishing companion.

Beyond a bend in the river we came upon the first human habitation I had seen in days. I experienced a shock of recognition that was almost uncanny, as though I had lived here in a previous life; and yet I had never seen anything exactly like this big cabin with its huge stone fireplace, rambling veranda, and green lawn sloping to the water. If Rascal and I were determined to live in the woods, here was the home we wanted.

I realized sadly, however, that wishing won't make it so. This cabin *must* belong to someone, and a fairly wealthy owner at that. As we came around a clump of willows, there he was, fishing his own trout pool with a split bamboo fly rod which he handled as gracefully as an orchestra conductor handles his baton.

He was a tall, spare man, browned by the sun and quietly intent upon his fishing. His old felt hat was decorated with trout flies. He was smoking a pipe and seemed completely at peace with the world.

I held Rascal in my arms so that he would not interrupt the performance, and we watched for several minutes, unnoticed by the fisherman.

It is fascinating to watch a good fly caster, and this man was an expert. It seemed almost impossible that with his wand of split bamboo he could direct a weightless lure with such precision that he could drop it on the water fifty feet downstream, within inches of any target, the fly lighting upon the pool as gently as though it were indeed a living insect.

On each back cast he lifted the lure and line high behind him, then with split-second timing brought forward the tip of his rod, sending the fly swiftly downstream to its destination. On each forward cast he stripped extra line from the reel until his fly was reaching the edge of a boulder at the foot of the pool, a good sixty feet below the gravel bar on which he was standing.

Then it happened, just as the fisherman had planned. There was a heavy swirl as the trout left his haven below the boulder, a tremendous surge, then a leap clear of the water.

I suppose we should have been cheering for that fish, making such a gallant fight for his life. But Rascal and I were primitive, as eager as the fly caster to bring the big trout to net. We ran down the path to the gravel bar to be nearer the scene of action as the tall, calm fisherman patiently played the fish. The rod bent like a bow during the lunges, easing to a gentle arc as the trout ran upstream.

Although busy with his fish, the angler looked up and smiled when he saw his visitors. But I knew enough not to talk at such a moment. The line cut swift figures across the surface of the water like an ice skater in motion, and once again the trout broke water, throwing spray into the sunlight.

"Pretty fair brown," the fisherman said.

"It's enormous."

"Not for a brown trout; get them anywhere up to twelve pounds in the Brule."

When the fish began to tire, the fisherman pointed to his long-handled net lying on the bar. "Want to slip it under him, son?"

"But I might lose him!"

"Wouldn't matter much—lots more where he came from."

I had used a landing net often, and knew that one must be careful not to scare the fish. The technique is to slip the net very gently behind and below him, and bring it forward and upward with a swift, smooth movement.

But Rascal knew none of these subtleties. In his eagerness he paced the beach, and when the trout showed his back above water, Rascal pounced. This sent the fish surging to the bottom of the pool. I gave Rascal a light slap on the nose which sent him whimpering up a little tree, talking and scolding about the injustice of it all.

Instead of being angry, the fisherman began laughing until he had to take his pipe from his mouth.

"It might have cost you your trout," I said apologetically.

"What's one trout more or less?"

"Well, this one's a beauty," I said as I brought the net under him. "I'll bet he weighs almost three pounds."

"Would you like him, sonny?"

"I couldn't take your best fish."

"Best fish?" The big man started laughing again. "You and your 'coon come up to the cabin. I'll show you a real trout."

As we went in through the big plank door of the cabin, I again had the weird feeling that I knew this place—the great room with its granite fireplace, the shelves of books, the bearskin rug! If I hadn't lived here (and of course I hadn't) I must have dreamed it in detail.

Bert Bruce—for that was his name—wanted to show me the eleven-pound trout mounted above the mantel so realistically that it seemed alive, rising to the brilliant Royal Coachman—the very fly which had been his undoing. When I held Rascal up to see this magnificent brown trout, he reached for the splash of crimson which had also lured the fish. My raccoon was proving much too interested in trout flies.

What struck me immediately about this cabin was its air of livability. The great pine logs—some of them forty feet in length—had been peeled and varnished. The pegged plank floor was of white oak, easy to clean. Comfortable chairs, a long table beneath windows overlooking the river, gasoline lamps—everything perfect for an evening of reading beside a birchwood fire.

Mr. Bruce hung his fly-decorated hat on a peg, well above the reach of Rascal, and, while my raccoon investigated at floor level, showed me his cabinet of flies. I had never seen anything like it—jars of preserved insects, netted from this valley, filled an entire shelf. These were the models for the artificial flies which this angler tied himself.

The small drawers, containing the many materials used to make the flies, might have been those of a jeweler. Within each drawer he kept a separate treasure, well protected from moths with balls of camphor. The hackles for his flies were largely from game cocks, red, ginger, and grizzled. These he imported from England. He trapped his own red foxes and rabbits, to make from their under fur the thoraxes or bodies of his flies, which were firmly banded to the hook with gold or silver wire as fine as a cobweb. The tails of the flies were the slenderest of feather barbs, and the wings were usually small feathers from a starling.

Then, with slight hesitation, he showed me the contents of the only drawer which was locked. I immediately realized it contained the feathers of a wood duck.

"I've shot only one in my life," he said. "I need these feathers—can't tie some flies without them."

There they lay, gleaming and radiant, the plumage of the most beautiful bird in North America.

While I was learning about the art of tying flies, Rascal had found the bearskin rug. The head was mounted with the ferocious mouth wide open, and Rascal was sidling up, as cautious as a cat, ready at any moment to leap back if the rug attacked him. I twitched the rug just once and Rascal nearly fell over backward. But his curiosity outweighed his caution and he soon returned, touching the bear's nose, running sensitive fingers over the fierce glass eyes. Convinced at last that the bear was not alive, he climbed aboard the massive head, proud to have won such a dangerous battle. Soon he was curled in a comfortable position on the skin of this great cousin. In another moment he was asleep.

"Do you live here all alone, Mr. Bruce?"

"Call me Bert," my host said. "Everybody else does. . . . Yes, I live alone. Can't stand womenfolks around—cranky clean."

"That's the way I feel," I said.

"Now you take my older sister. I live with her winters, and I like her. But when she comes up here she dusts and scrubs and changes curtains and moves furniture. Can't lay a book down on the table, she puts it right back on the shelf."

"I wish I had a cabin like this," I said.

"Well, son," Bert said, "you can't get anything in this world without working for it. I ran a sporting goods store in Chicago for thirty years. Sold out and retired. I come up here from early May to late October. But I had to earn the money first."

"I'd work all my life for a cabin like this," I said wistfully.

"How about a ham sandwich for you and your 'coon?"

"That would suit us just fine."

"Well, come along to the icehouse and we'll cut a big slice of ham."

I took Rascal with us to be sure he wouldn't get into mischief. And while we were in the icehouse, Bert had a good idea. He wanted to see how much Rascal weighed.

Taking his trout creel, he hung it from a scale permanently attached to one of the beams. Discounting the weight of the creel, he now lifted the amiable little raccoon into the wicker basket. Rascal weighed exactly four pounds and three ounces.

"How old is he?" Bert asked.

"Just about four months, I think."

"Coming along fine," Bert said, relighting his pipe. "Gaining just about a pound a month. He'll be a big husky fellow before he goes to sleep for the winter."

There wasn't any doubt about it. Bert Bruce was our friend.

It seemed scarcely possible that two weeks had fled so swiftly. But one afternoon my father returned to tell me that the court case had been settled and that the following day would be our last on the Brule. For the first time since we had come to the north woods, I lay awake for a while that evening, listening to the soughing of the wind high in the pines, realizing sadly that we must now return to civilization.

I went to sleep with the happier thought that we still had one precious day, and I was determined to make the most of it.

Next morning we took our fishpoles and started downstream to Bert's cabin. It was cool enough to make us grateful for our sweaters. The grass and low bushes in the little clearings were hung with spider webs, seeded with pearls of dew, and a few birches were exchanging their summer green for the pale gold of early autumn.

My father and Bert had become good friends. On several evenings they had talked about Indians—a mutual passion: the Winnebagos, the Chippewas, the Crees, the Teton Sioux, and many others. While Rascal and I lay on the bearskin rug, Indians swirled noiselessly around us through the flickering firelight—dancing their war dances, hunting and fishing, moving forlornly to their reservations.

For our pleasure on this final day, Bert had offered us the use of his canoe, and we were eager to try it. The Brule is mostly navigable by light craft from this cabin down to Lake Superior, and there are several excellent trout pools on these lower reaches almost certain to produce big fish.

Bert saw us safely afloat, bid us farewell and good luck, and waved from his gravel bar. We rounded a bend in the rapids below his pool, and cascaded through a tunnel of evergreens.

My father was at the stern and I in the forward seat. Rascal was convinced that he was the pilot. He stood at the prow, peering downstream as might an animated figurehead, sniffing the breeze, watching the river, and occasionally turning to give us brief instructions. As always, he loved speed and a slight sense of danger, chirring with the most satisfaction when we were running white water.

My father had purchased his first canoe nearly half a century before from a Winnebago Indian. He was excellent, guiding us with swift strokes, or the rudderlike action of the trailing paddle. I was also a competent performer, but less adept at the stern than near the prow.

The canoe itself was as safe as a rowboat, four feet shorter than the one I was building, and twice as wide. It was a handsome craft, riding the water like a swan and taking us lightly over the shallows where trout lay on the clean gravel, nosing upward against the current. They were almost as invisible as a woodcock among brown leaves.

There were very few good fishing places along the first quarter mile below Bert's pool, and I did not put aside my paddle to take my rod until we had passed the second bend.

Here we found water so peaceful that we could cast our bucktail flies at leisure while letting the canoe drift slowly with the current. A noisy kingfisher disputed our right to his domain, darting angrily across our path, his crest as erect as the war bonnet of an Indian. For perhaps thirty seconds a mink watched us from a sand bar, appearing from the underbrush and disappearing again so quickly that we might have doubted our senses had not all three of us seen him clearly. My father hooked a small trout but returned it to the stream.

As we left the pool we again took our paddles to dart precipitously down another chute. Guiding this craft among the boulders, I thought happily of my own canoe at home which some day would be ready for the water. My raccoon and I would be afloat every possible moment.

About a mile below Bert's cabin, Rascal's sensitive nose caught a scent that spelled danger, and he trilled a warning. Just then my father and I saw a blueberry patch that looked as though it had been hit by a small cyclone.

A little farther down the stream, a hollow tree had been ripped open as though by lightning, with shreds of bark and rotten wood and dark honeycomb strewn over a gravel bar. There could be no doubt about it. This was the work of a bear.

Talking softly now, and paddling quietly, we progressed cautiously over tranquil water around a wide bend in the stream. And there they were, at the foot of the pool, a mother black bear and her two cubs. She had just tossed a big trout to her offspring from the rapids below this pool, and the cubs were fighting over the fish, snarling and snapping.

Rascal's high trill diverted her from her fishing, and with a deep-throated growl she stood her ground for a few moments, eyeing us angrily. Rascal didn't need to be cautioned against swimming to meet these big, rough cousins of his. He stood transfixed at the prow, fascinated but trembling.

The bear spoke sharply to her cubs and plunged into the willows and aspens with a great crackling of brush. And her obedient young raced after her. They disappeared as completely as the mink, and soon there was silence.

"Well, Sterling, you've seen your first bears."

"And my first deer, and my first porcupine."

Nothing could top this experience, I thought, but at the next trout pool there was one to match it. I overcast the pool into the rapids below and was retrieving my bucktail in an erratic manner to avoid a snag when a smashing strike bent my pole as though it were of willow. My line was taut, and the fish had hooked himself solidly on the wet fly and seemed inclined to take it all the way down-river to Lake Superior.

My father backed water to hold the canoe steady against the slight current running through the pool, and I did my best to keep the trout from tangling the line in the half-submerged log in the rapids.

Other fish can fight, but there is nothing quite like big trout for style and grace and courage—as though they drew strength from the whole wilderness. Rascal was as excited as I, chattering and chirring.

Changing tactics, the fish made a dash upstream into our pool. I reeled in slack line as rapidly as possible to keep the needed tension on the hook. For one dreadful moment I thought I had lost him, but a few more twists of the reel showed me that the trout was still solidly hooked, deep in the Brule. In another few moments he surfaced, saw the canoe, and started a wide, circling run upstream.

My father swung the prow one hundred and eighty degrees to give me the best chance to play my fish, which now broke water in a great gleaming leap. Rascal's high trill was like a cheer of praise.

When at last my father slipped the net under my fish and brought him into the canoe I found that I had a fine brown trout, one of the largest I would ever catch in a lifetime of fishing. By the scales in my tackle box he weighed just over four pounds.

"He's as big as you are, Rascal," I said with delight.

"He's a beauty, Sterling."

"Shall I try for more?"

"If you like."

But as I put my fish on wet ferns in my creel, I decided I would leave all the other trout in the stream for that day. With pulse still beating a tattoo, I took my paddle and we began the tough return journey against the current.

Somewhere it must all be recorded, as insects are captured in amber—that day on the river: transcribed in Brule water, written on the autumn air, safe at least in my memory.

That was the best trout I have ever eaten. It made a feast that evening for the three of us. But soon after dousing our campfire a wind arose, roaring through the pines, and driving the cold rain like sleet through the dripping forest. We hastily packed everything in the car, put up the side curtains, and spent an uncomfortable night huddled on the seats of the Oldsmobile. Next day we started home through air washed clean by the storm. We were tired and damp, but replenished by two weeks among the pines of our magnificent north country.

v: *September*

WHEN we curved up our drive, Edgar Allan Poe came swooping down from the Methodist belfry shouting, "What fun! What fun!" Wowser, who had thought he was totally deserted, came bouncing from the barn, leaped to put his paws on my shoulders, and knocked me flat on my back in the grass where he lovingly washed my face with his big tongue.

Rascal and the crow were soon fighting over something, and Wowser stopped licking me long enough to put an end to the squabble.

It was a wonderful homecoming.

Sweet corn was no longer an issue, being dry in the husk. But I had made a promise and was honor-bound to keep it. I couldn't postpone indefinitely the collar and leash, nor the building of the cage. We had been granted our reprieve and now must face our problems.

One of those problems was money. I had earned and saved enough to buy one Liberty Bond, but my available supply of ready cash was very low. I counted the quarters, dimes, nickels, and pennies in my earthenware crock and decided that if I bought the leash and collar, and the lumber and chicken wire for the cage, it would set me back about six months in purchasing canvas to cover my canoe. And that meant the canoe would have to stay in the living room another winter.

Not one of the boys I knew was granted an allowance or would even think of asking his father for a loan. I felt fortunate to be permitted to keep the money I earned from mowing lawns and selling my garden produce.

I took four precious quarters from the crock, put Rascal in the basket of my bicycle, and pedaled slowly and sadly downtown. Buying a collar and leash for my pet raccoon was like buying a ball and chain for a dear friend. But I thought it would be wise to have Rascal's approval and assistance; it might lessen his terror when he found that his freedom had vanished.

We stopped at Shadwick's Harness and Leather Emporium, which smelled delightfully of tanned leather, saddle soap, and harness oil. It was a perfect place for Rascal to browse, examining the stirrups of both Western and English saddles, the brass buckles on the work harnesses, and the exquisite silver mountings on a set of driving harnesses being made for the local banker's high-stepping team.

Garth Shadwick, like his father before him, was a craftsman in leather whose skill was known as far away as the county seat and the state capital. He made handsome leather luggage, custom-fitted riding boots, and engraved book bindings. But most of his trade was in harnesses; and harness-making was a profession threatened by the automobile.

At this moment Mr. Shadwick had a jeweler's glass in his right eye and was engraving scrolled initials on a silver nameplate. I would not interrupt him at such a moment, and waited patiently until he took the glass from his eye and looked up from his work.

"Well, Sterling?"

"We don't want to bother you, Mr. Shadwick . . ."

"Boys and 'coons don't bother me," the harness-maker said.

He returned to his engraving for several minutes, then tossed it aside and exploded, "It's these gol-danged automobiles, smelly, noisy, dirty things, scaring horses right off the road . . . ruin a man's business . . . Well, son, speak up. What is it you want?"

"I want a collar for Rascal," I said, fighting the stinging moisture in my eyes, "and a braided leash to match. . . . And they're making me build a cage to lock him up."

"Gol-danged buzzards," the harness-maker said. "Cage for a little 'coon like that? Going after boys and 'coons now, are they? . . . You want his name engraved on a silver plate on the collar?"

"I haven't got much money," I said hesitantly. "But that would be wonderful. . . . His name is Rascal."

"Come here, Rascal, and let me measure your neck,"

Garth Shadwick said, leaning over to pat my complacent pet.

"You don't need to measure him, Mr. Shadwick. Here's a string that's just the right length for the collar, with knots where the holes and the buckle should be, and allowing a little for when he gets bigger."

The harness-maker came as near to smiling as I had ever seen him. With swift precision he went to work on a strong, light collar of pliable, golden-brown calfskin, about half an inch wide. He used his smallest awl to make the holes and his smallest needle and lightest waxed thread. Then he went to his safe and brought out a tiny silver buckle which he sewed to the collar with almost invisible stitches. It was the sort of work he would have done if asked to make a harness for a fairy coach. Finally he put his glass to his eye, and on a very small silver nameplate inscribed "Rascal" in a fine Spencerian script.

"That's the most beautiful raccoon collar I ever saw in my life," I said.

"It's the only raccoon collar you ever saw—" the harness-maker chuckled gruffly—"and the only one I ever made. . . . Better try it for size."

I wasn't certain that Rascal would like to have the collar put around his neck, but I couldn't hurt Mr. Shadwick's feelings. I let the little raccoon feel it and smell it first, telling him it was his newest treasure. Rascal liked the shining buckle and nameplate and the texture of the soft leather.

Finally I slipped it around his neck, and to my surprise he didn't struggle or try to nip me. Instead he sat up on his square little bottom and began feeling the collar the way a woman sometimes fingers her pearls.

Mr. Shadwick brought the floor mirror used for viewing riding boots. And Rascal, who had never before seen his mirror image, became greatly excited. He wondered what other raccoon was being fitted for a collar this morning. First he bumped his nose trying to get through the mirror. Then, talking and trilling, he raced around behind the glass to meet the other raccoon, who of course wasn't there. Back he came, completely mystified, but still entranced. Finally he gave it up as a puzzle too deep for his small brain and merely sat and viewed himself, chirring happily.

Making the leash took a little longer, but again the harness maker worked with amazing dexterity. He cut six very slender strips of the same calfskin, and began the most elaborate job of braiding I had ever seen. His fingers worked so swiftly I could not see which strands went over and which went under and through. The finished leash, inch by perfect inch, was as slim as the tip of my steel fishing rod.

At my end of the leash he fastened a silver harness ring, at the other end a snap to attach to the collar.

I knew that I didn't have enough money in my earthenware crock to pay for such a collar and leash complete with silver fittings. So I put my four quarters on Mr. Shadwick's work bench and said it was a down payment and that I would bring him something every week for the next six months.

The harness-maker gazed off through the window the

way Rascal often did—his mind going back, perhaps, to his own boyhood when there weren't any gol-danged automobiles to ruin the finest profession in the world.

"Why, son," he said, "I'd be cheating you if I took more than twenty-five cents for that leash and collar. Now get along with your little 'coon. I've got work to do."

There had been an overcast when we had started downtown that morning. But the sun was shining brightly as we pedaled homeward.

The opening of school was postponed for a month in the autumn of 1918. With so many young men away at war, the women and older children tried to fill their places on the farms around Brailsford Junction.

In this rich tobacco region, the crop is harvested in September—late enough to avoid "shed burn," but early enough to avoid frost. This is heavy work—chopping the tobacco stalks, spudding these plants on laths, and hanging the tobacco in the sheds to dry. I was too slight to be of much assistance in the harvest field, but I continued to produce food in my war garden—bushels of carrots, beets, and potatoes.

I used my garden as a justification for delaying the building of Rascal's cage. But I knew that his imprisonment could not be postponed forever, particularly after he developed a craving for a new nocturnal delight, the grapes hanging in purple clusters in nearby arbors. Rascal also sampled apples of many varieties—Jonathans, Winesaps, Tolman Sweets. And he was growing increasingly casual about obeying my imperative *trill,* which meant as he well knew, "Come down from that tree, you bad raccoon!"

I came to the reluctant conclusion that I would have to buy the materials and start constructing the cage. Taking my small hoard of coins from the earthenware crock, I snapped the leash on Rascal and walked down Albion Street toward Cy Jenkins' lumber yard. My raccoon had been introduced to his leash so gradually that he no longer strained against it painfully.

Considering my mission, I found it hard to enjoy this season which had always given me so much pleasure: the yellow elm leaves drifting down, the first flash of crimson in the maples.

Cy Jenkins had cheated me when I had bought lumber for my canoe. But he was so eager to see Rascal caged that he now pretended to be giving me a bargain on two-by-fours and chicken wire. He merely asked how much money I had and took it all.

"Comes out right to the penny," he said.

The old miser added one other concession, promising to deliver the material by truck on the following morning if I would start building the cage on its arrival.

I stopped at the post office to get our mail, and found a letter from Herschel addressed to me. My fingers trembled as I opened it. I had dreamed several times that he had been wounded, and I had been reading Arthur Guy Empey's *Over the Top*, a crude but vivid book about the war. In every scene I imagined Herschel.

In one persistent dream I saw him leading a reconnaissance squad into no-man's land at night, flattening himself as star shells burst, and making his way through barbed-wire entanglements where corpses dangled grotesquely. Much later I learned that he had made scores of such excursions between the lines.

Censorship made communication almost impossible in World War I, and Herschel's letter merely sent his love and confirmed the fact that he was unwounded. I remember one sentence in particular because it was typical of his wry good humor:

"Send me some Paris garters, Sterling. They claim in their ads that 'No metal can touch you.'"

The fact that Herschel was still alive and unhurt, and that Rascal and I still had one afternoon before I must start building the cage, raised my spirits considerably. I made jelly sandwiches for the two of us, and we climbed the cleats I had nailed to the oak tree, taking with us our picnic lunch and a copy of *Westward Ho*.

High in our favorite crotch, we ate and I read, fascinated by the adventures of Amyas Leigh. Rascal meanwhile indulged in a favorite pastime of raccoons, sunbathing on a lofty limb. He lay flat on his fat little belly on a branch he could comfortably embrace, letting all four legs dangle over the sides in easy balance. His muzzle pointed upstream on the bough, and his handsome ringed tail lay straight behind him. And there he dozed for hours, absorbing the healing sunshine of September as though he were storing up warmth for the long, cold season ahead.

I was equally happy, and quite as lost to the world,

as I sailed the Spanish Main with Amyas, followed him into the forest to find the beautiful white girl Ayacanora, and moved with mounting excitement toward the defeat of the Spanish Armada. We were tree-dwellers, my raccoon and I, and we rather wished we would never have to set foot on earth again.

Hunger brought us down at last, however, My father was in Montana on ranch business, so Rascal and I ate whatever we pleased for supper, and then climbed our tree once again to watch the stars come out. J told him some of the things my mother had told me about those distant suns, arranged in their shining constellations. Then I had a sad but happy thought. If Ursa Major, the Great Bear, was my constellation, Ursa Minor, the Little Bear, was by natural right Rascal's constellation. Long years after we were both gone, there we still would be, swimming across the midnight sky together.

There were two things I must do: plan the cage carefully, and convince Rascal that it would be a pleasure to live in his new home.

I had been observing him closely for the last few days to discover which part of the back yard he enjoyed the most. There could be no doubt about his preference—it was an area about twelve feet square which extended from the base of the oak tree, below his hole, to the side of the barn. This included a smooth expanse of grass and white clover, and my bait pool with its running water and constant supply of minnows.

Just as I had let Rascal become slowly acquainted with

his collar and then his leash, I now invited his help in constructing the cage. When the wire and two-by-fours arrived, I laid out the square, dug holes for the posts, and also sank a six-inch trench along each side for pegging down the bottom edge of the wire.

Rascal enjoyed all this activity without understanding its true meaning. He reached into each excavation, crawled back and forth through the central tunnel in the rolls of chicken wire, fished languidly in the bait pool, or merely went to sleep in the grass.

My father sent a postcard from Montana saying he would not return for another ten days or two weeks. Fortunately we ran a charge account at the meat market and at one of the groceries. But to raise money for staples and hinges I had to dig and sell two more bushels of my potatoes. I was somewhat lonesome and very grateful for Rascal's companionship night and day.

Possibly I could have built the cage in less time had I not been aware of its purpose. However, the posts were soon set and, in another day, the framework nailed together. It was a cube twelve feet square which gave easy access to Rascal's hole in the oak tree. It also encompassed the bait pool, using twelve feet of the barn along the eastern side. I had to fasten wire securely across the top of this cube, knowing that Rascal could climb any fence ever built. I used an old screen door for the principal entrance, nailing chicken wire to the frame and hinging the door to a sturdy post. But during the several days I spent building the cage, I was careful not to close this exit. Never for a moment did Rascal feel penned in.

117

I fed him his favorite foods within the wire, always dreading the day when I must hook the door.

It seemed to me a wicked thing, to take a wild raccoon kitten from the woods—a little animal who loved speed and adventure and exploration—and to imprison him like an animal at the zoo. I had seen the big cats and the bears pace up and down their cages in hopeless misery. Would Rascal yearn like that for his lost freedom?

He *must* have more space, I thought, and more shelter!

Then I had a small inspiration. I hurried to my work bench to get a compass, brace-and-bit, and keyhole saw. Making sure that my calculations were right, I drew a circle on the side of the barn, big enough for a raccoon but too small for a dog. I then bored four holes within the circle, and using my slender saw cut a neat opening into a long-disused box stall inside the barn. Finally I sanded the edges of this doorway so that it would not scratch Rascal; and I showed him the net result.

Rascal loved holes of all sizes, from crayfish holes to be explored with a sensitive paw, to holes such as this one, big enough to crawl into. While I put fresh straw in the box stall, and enclosed it in chicken wire, my raccoon spent most of his time going in and out of his pleasant little door. His home was becoming more attractive day by day.

He still didn't understand, however, that I was building him a prison. And every time the neighbors asked when I would lock him up, I said, "Maybe tomorrow."

The most exciting event in Brailsford Junction each September was the Irish Picnic and Horse Fair. It was always held on a Saturday somewhat earlier in the month than the County Fair at Janesville to which many of the race horses and exhibitors later gravitated.

I do not know why it was called the "Irish Picnic," since a very small percentage of our town was Irish. But they did possess most of the good trotters and pacers of our area, and in all probability had instituted these races which now attracted spectators by the hundreds.

Mike Conway, our neighbor to the west, owned a terrific trotter, a spirited stallion that had sired several of the most likely colts and fillies in the county. Early on the morning of any Irish Picnic, Mike was to be seen currying Donnybrook to a satin sheen, washing the sulky, and oiling his racing harness.

Donnybrook seemed as aware as his master that this was the great day. His whinny could be heard at a considerable distance by interested mares, and he frisked about his pasture, kicking up his heels and tossing his head.

Some race horses have a beloved dog or cat for a companion. Donnybrook had developed a strong affection for Rascal. Whenever my raccoon climbed one of the posts of the neat white fence around the paddock, the black stallion immediately became gentle, changing his shrill whinny to a soft whicker. While Rascal waited on the fencepost, Donnybrook would trot over to greet him. The raccoon always ran his small hands over the big velvet muzzle, fingering the bright rings of the halter.

Naturally Rascal and I would be cheering for Donnybrook in any race he might ever run.

Across the street on this same morning, Reverend Thurman was tuning up the carburetor and making other last-minute adjustments on his Model T roadster. He was bellowing hymns which were explosively interrupted whenever he pinched a finger or dropped a wrench.

Mike Conway and Gabriel Thurman had never been the best of friends, but in recent weeks their feud had taken a new turn. Mike loved horses and hated automobiles almost as ardently as his friend Garth Shadwick. Thurman was terrified of horses, but entranced with automobiles.

Mike wouldn't admit that he was afraid of anything. But the fact remained that he had never taken a ride in an automobile until a recent day when the minister had offered him a lift in his Ford. Mike silently asked the protection of St. Patrick, stepped into the shivering, shaking, self-propelled chariot of destruction, and they were off.

On every possible occasion Gabriel blew his horn—a Klaxon, nerve-racking enough to frighten every horse on the block. As he turned from Albion into Fulton—the principal business street—the minister pulled down the gas lever and went roaring through the traffic with satanic delight, while Mike muttered a fervent "Hail Mary" and turned a patriotic green.

Mike made it a point to return the favor. Two days later he hitched his training cart to Donnybrook and offered Thurman a ride across town to his church. The minister, who wasn't entirely dim-witted, said thank you just the same. Mike taunted him a little about his courage, and Gabriel flushed a bright pink and climbed into the cart.

The trot down Albion was not too frightening, but the established course was Fulton Street—as both men knew. In front of Pringle's store, Mike touched up the ever-willing stallion. By the time they reached the Tobacco Exchange Bank, Donnybrook had hit his top speed. Thurman didn't start calling upon Jehovah until they were abreast of the Badger Ice Cream Parlor. But long before they reached the Monarch Laboratories—which produced a nerve tonic for just such occasions—his eyes were rolling and he was screaming, "Help! Murder! Runaway horse! Let me out, you fool!"

The entire town knew all about both rides, and the best-informed gossips insisted that Conway and Thurman had made some sort of wager—highly improper on the part of a minister—and that the mysterious payoff might come during the day of the Irish Picnic.

I was as curious as everyone else. So, taking Rascal on my shoulder, I crossed the street to Thurman's parsonage where he continued to work on his car.

"I'd be glad to polish your brass radiator," I said.

Reverend Thurman glared at me and at Rascal.

"The best way to polish a radiator is with a 'coon pelt. And if that animal of yours ever invades my property again . . ."

"You wouldn't do that to my pet raccoon!"

"Oh yes, indeed; I certainly would," said the terrible-tempered minister of the Gospel. "I'll tack his hide right up in the woodshed. Thought you were going to lock him in his cage, like you promised."

"In a few days," I said. "You can see I've got him on a leash."

"Step in the right direction," Thurman granted.

I knew it was impolite, but my curiosity was now quite out of control. I was slightly shocked to hear myself asking. "What's your bet with Mike Conway, Reverend Thurman?"

"Bet?" Thurman shouted. "What bet? Ministers never bet. Now you and your 'coon get out of here, and stay out."

We returned to our front porch, and Rascal and I sat in wicker chairs watching a veritable parade. Our street was the direct route to the fair grounds, and all the exhibits and livestock, the race horses and the automobiles must come past us in review, as though we were judges or privileged guests.

There were always a few well-groomed hunters and hackney ponies, thoroughbreds and Tennessee walking horses, five-gaiters and other pampered creatures moving with pride and grace toward assured white, red, or blue ribbons. But our region was one of working prosperity rather than effortless luxury, so most of our beautiful horses were of the draft breeds.

We had massive Belgians, often weighing more than a ton and standing seventeen hands high, Suffolks, Clydesdales, and Percherons. In the pulling contests these tremendous and faithful animals were so brave and loyal to their masters that I could not watch them long in their heartbreaking performances.

Apparently they would soon be outmoded by the other forms of locomotion passing our front-row seat—automobiles of every kind from Fords to White Steamers and twin-six Packards. The sulkies, surreys, and neat green farm wagons, with gleaming red wheels, moved very slowly by comparison to any automobile.

My father was still in Montana, so this year he would not be with me viewing the exhibits and watching the races. I raided my earthenware crock for my last handful of small silver, snapped the leash on Rascal, mounted my bicycle, and we were on our way.

The world was sparkling and cool that bright September morning. The dust had been settled during the night by a sprinkle of rain—not enough to make a muddy track, just enough to put ozone in the air and dew on the grass. Whistling any tune that came into my head, I pedaled happily toward the fair grounds with Rascal in the basket.

In the traffic were additional guarantees of a good day: the pie wagon, the ice cream truck which also carried many cases of root beer, the popcorn and crackerjack wagon, and a balloon-man riding a bicycle and blowing an enchanting little whistle that lured children as surely as the pipe of the Pied Piper. From up ahead within the fair grounds, we could hear the steam calliope playing: "Come Josephine In My Flying Machine."

And now the bright tents and the white buildings came

123

into view and we could hear the happy buzz and murmur of the crowd already gathering. Yes, this was certainly the day of the Irish Picnic, worth coming miles to see.

I put my bicycle in the bicycle rack under the grandstand and with Rascal on my shoulder began to tour the grounds. We saw all the canned goods, quilts, and other fancywork in the homecraft department.

In another building we admired the huge pumpkins, Hubbard squashes, and melons, the seed corn, apples, and grapes. It was a good thing that I had Rascal on a leash. He wanted to run his avid hands over everything he saw, like a woman shopper at a fire sale. In the case of the prize-winning bunch of grapes, I restrained him just in time.

On visiting the livestock building Rascal walked the top rail of the pens, utterly confident and unafraid. Calves and colts came over to say hello. The fattened lambs were also gentle. But a big Poland China sow with her autumn litter was menacing. And a Merino ram charged the fence on which Rascal was standing, moving like an oncoming locomotive and crashing his big curled horns into the wooden partition. Rascal would have been thrown into the pen by this heavy jolt if I had not literally dragged him from danger by his leash.

We were more careful after that, as we visited the horse pavilion to see again, at closer range, the beautiful animals we had seen passing our house earlier in the morning.

Most of the horses were not entered in any special event except the grand parade around the race track. They were judged in their pavilion by three craggy and serious horsemen brought in for the occasion; and some of the blue, red, and white ribbons had already been awarded. But out in the racing stables were the handsome trotters and pacers we would later watch in action. There were two-year-olds—both colts and fillies—who would compete in the Junior Classic. They were high-spirited young things with fire and mischief in their eyes, and I kept Rascal well back from the paddock doors. Most of the three-year-olds were better behaved. And, of course, there was Donnybrook, who whickered his greeting and nuzzled Rascal affectionately. In two of the last three years he had won the Senior Classic. And I think he knew that we were pulling for him.

It was pure delight to be showing Rascal all this for the first time, and he was constantly interested in all that he saw. We rode the merry-go-round together, Rascal sitting ahead of me on the wooden pony, going gaily up and down, round and round. He wanted a second ride, but I had to be careful of my dimes or we would never get through the day without going bankrupt. We couldn't resist the Ferris wheel, however. It was the biggest one that had ever come to the Irish Picnic, and when we reached the top we could see all the way to the village of Albion far across the marshes. Height didn't frighten either of us, and it was a little like flying to soar upward and come swooping down again.

Rascal would gladly have ridden all day, and so would I, but the silver in my pocket was disappearing far too rapidly.

It didn't cost anything to enter the three-legged race. But when I saw some of those long-legged fourteen-year-olds teaming up, I knew that Oscar Sunderland and I didn't have a chance. Instead we decided to enter another free event soon to begin, the pie-eating contest.

Gabbling happily about Rascal and the coming muskrat season, we walked toward the long plank table and adjoining benches laid out with twenty blueberry pies.

"I seen a mink track," Oscar said. "Lives in the tile that drains Mud Lake. You got your traps oiled?"

"Not yet. But I sent to St. Louis for our fur catalogues."

"Boy, we're going to make a fortune this fall. We're going to be filthy rich."

"I could use some money," I admitted. "I'm just about stone broke."

"Gee, so am I. Flat busted . . . Say, look at that pie."

"Not as good as your mother makes."

"She does make good pie at that," Oscar admitted. "Mom's all right."

We sat down on either side of the table, ten boys on each side. Our hands were tied behind our backs, and while we awaited the starting gun we shouted happy insults at each other. The object of this messy contest was to eat the full-sized pie faster than any other contestant. You had to eat it with your face, and pull the pie tin back with your teeth if it started slipping beyond reach. I noticed a knot in the wide plank that might be helpful. If I could maneuver the pie tin right up against that knot, I could really dig in.

Then I discovered that I was directly across the table

from Slammy Stillman, and I knew this would be the toughest pie-eating contest I had ever entered. Slammy was the biggest, greediest, meanest twelve-year-old in town. We hated each other with a fine, soul-satisfying hatred born of many fist fights in which I was always outweighed and outslugged. But by boyhood rules you could never refuse to fight.

We glared at each other balefully. This was a grudge fight to the last blueberry and the last crumb of pie crust.

Bang! We were off with a good juicy plunge through the crust and deep into the berries. The knot in the plank helped a little, but not enough. It held the pie tin for about three good slurps, then let it slip. There was so much commotion, noise, and splattering of blueberries, with some boys practically lying on the table trying to re- cover their pie tins, that it was hard to see who was win- ning. The crowd around us was roaring with laughter, but it wasn't very funny to us. We were desperate, exas- perated, covered with blueberries, and breathing hard. Everybody wanted the three-dollar grand prize, not to mention the glory and the blue ribbon.

I was practically certain that only Slammy Stillman was ahead of me, and I didn't see how I could ever catch up. Then my best friend came to my rescue. Rascal knew all about pies, and he loved blueberries. He leaped to the table and started helping me eat my pie, licking it up at a wonderful rate. Best of all, he was working from the other side of the pie, adding five-and-one-half pounds of raccoon to the resistance already supplied by the knot. My tin scarcely slipped at all.

Slammy Stillman was the first to notice. He was completely infuriated. This character, who never abided by any rule, started screaming, "Cheater, cheater, look at that cheater!"

While Slammy was yelling he couldn't eat pie. Rascal and I were gaining on him fast. The judges were laughing so hard they couldn't catch their breath to shout a ruling.

Rascal and I came in strong on the last lick, an eighth of a pie ahead of our nearest competitor, who luckily was Oscar Sunderland.

Neither Spaulding nor Hoyle has ever published a handbook on pie-eating contests, and the judges went into a huddle that became vociferous. Rascal and I were partially disqualified. Oscar got the three dollars and the blue ribbon, which made me happy because Oscar was my trapping partner and as nearly penniless as I. But I received the consolation prize, a real league baseball autographed by every member of our local team.

Slammy would have been red in the face if he hadn't been completely blue in the face. All day long he grumbled and threatened, shouting "Cheater" whenever he saw me and my raccoon. It was a delicious victory.

The September sun was directly overhead. But for some reason Rascal and I did not respond to the dinner bells being rung by warm and hearty matrons serving food in several denominational tents. On the Methodist menu were roast chicken with dressing, three vegetables, and blueberry pie. It was this last item which convinced us that we didn't need a noonday meal.

At two in the afternoon the horse races began. A beautiful bay filly from Janesville nosed out the favorite colt from Madison in the Junior Classic. She had the movements of a Swiss watch, lifting her feet proudly, her muscles rippling smoothly. After this upset, the three-year-olds performed more predictably, with a magnificent pacer from Stoughton breaking the track record for eight furlongs. As race followed race, however, the spectators asked each other, "Where is Donnybrook?"

Mike Conway was not tiring his black stallion.

Much as he enjoyed winning the Senior Classic, he had another aim in view today—the all-but-impossible hope that he could outrun a greater menace than any competing horse, in fact Gabriel Thurman's Model T.

There are probably no more than fifty trotters who have pulled a sulky one mile in two minutes. Possibly ninety pacers have achieved this immortality. Generally speaking, it takes a great horse in harness racing to speed one furlong in fifteen seconds, or one mile in two minutes.

Similarly (unless handled by a racing driver) few early Fords could top twice this speed— sixty miles an hour, or "a-mile-a-minute."

The mathematics of this race seemed obvious. A very fast trotter was matched against a well-attuned Ford. By any sensible odds, Reverend Gabriel Thurman should have been asked to drive his tin Lizzy four times around the half-mile oval while Donnybrook wheeled Mike Conway twice around this track.

129

All through the grandstand the news spread swiftly. Mike had bet that he could go twice around the track while Thurman and his Ford made a mere *three* rounds! There was one shrewd catch, however. Donnybrook needed no cranking, and Thurman must wait for the starting gun before cranking his Ford, jumping into his roadster, and streaking off after the stallion and his master.

Mike Conway had watched the impatient and impetuous Gabriel Thurman crank his Ford on many occasions. He knew that Thurman always took reckless chances in three departments. He placed the gas and also the spark lever much too low. When aggravated he always jerked the choke wire (which emerged at the left of the crank), thus flooding his carburetor. Mike was no mechanic, but he had often used his stop watch on Thurman's futile attempts to start his car.

Gabriel Thurman was aware of his impetuosity. He knew that in his eagerness to make his Ford rumble and roar he caused backfires that nearly broke his arm. He was being tremendously cautious, putting the spark and gas barely below the permissible level, and promising himself he would not touch the ring attached to the wire that primed the carburetor.

The flag was lowered, the barrier raised, and Mike and Donnybrook were off in a flash. It was sheer joy to watch that stallion lift his white-stockinged feet. Mike rode comfortably on the seat of the sulky, as much a part of his trotter as though he had been astride.

Gabriel Thurman gave the crank a whirl, and was

nearly knocked into the dust by the backfire. He rushed to his steering wheel, adjusted gas and spark, and tried once again. A very small "pop" created such exasperation that the minister pulled the priming wire with a desperate yank. The carburetor flooded until it dripped gas beneath the car.

By this time Mike Conway and Donnybrook had completed a full round of the track and had only one more to go. By luck rather than skill, Thurman now started his Ford. And off he blasted, sounding his Klaxon and pulling his gas lever to the lowest notch. This was almost an even race, if the Ford could make sixty miles an hour while Donnybrook held thirty.

On the open road, Thurman might have won. But taking the curves without leaping the fence was his problem. Donnybrook crossed the finish line leading by two lengths, the indisputable winner.

There was one other reward for Rascal and for me. Donnybrook moved over to the fence where my raccoon was watching and waiting eagerly. With more than 1,000 spectators enjoying the sight, Donnybrook nuzzled Rascal, while Rascal ran his hands over the stallion's nose and bridle. Once again we had tasted victory.

I came home in the early evening to the empty house. I called the telegraph office in the railroad station to learn if my father had wired from Montana telling me when he was coming home. But of course he had sent no message.

I took Rascal to his cage, and sat for a long time talking to him and petting him while he ate his evening meal. Then, steeling myself to the dreadful deed, I stepped from the cage and closed the door behind me, hooking it firmly on the outside.

Rascal didn't understand what had happened at first. He came over to the door and asked me politely to open it and let him out. Then the thought suddenly struck him that he was trapped, caged, imprisoned. He ran swiftly around the square of wire, then into the barn, through the hole I had cut, and all over that inside enclosure, then back again, frantic now.

I went into the house to get away from his voice, but it came to me through the open windows—pleading, terrified—asking for me—telling me he loved me and had always trusted me.

After a while I couldn't stand it any longer and I went out and opened the wire door. He clung to me and cried and talked about it, asking that unanswerable question.

So I took him to bed with me and we both fell into a fitful sleep, touching each other again and again throughout the night for reassurance.

VI: *October*

RETURNING to school had always been a pleasure. It meant new pencils and composition books—the pencils smelling of cedar as you sharpened them. Most of the texts were dog-eared and scrawled with unfunny comments and crude drawings. But occasionally we were furnished two or three books fresh from the presses, fragrant of new paper and printers' ink. The beginning of this school year was particularly memorable because I was entering Junior High School.

The Senior High School pupils, who sat in the forward part of the main assembly hall, were disdainful of those of us who sat at the rear. But we realized that some day we would be as grand as they; and we had our own loyalties and interests which saved us from suffering too deeply the stigma of being both small and young.

At least two of my new teachers were greatly gifted.

Miss Stafford made English a delight. And Miss Whalen loved biology as my mother had loved it.

My only reluctance upon hearing the first schoolbell in October, 1918, was that I must end my summer with Rascal and lock him firmly in his chicken-wire mansion. I had moved Wowser's large doghouse to a position just outside Rascal's door. It would have been a brave boy or dog daring to risk intrusion upon my raccoon's privacy. Well aware of his trust, Wowser lay just outside the cage, his huge muzzle and deep, compassionate eyes turned toward the small prisoner just inside the wire. Rascal, reaching out to his shoulder, patted Wowser's nose, and the Saint Bernard invariably licked the little paw extended in friendship. When Rascal chirred or trilled, Wowser answered with a big, gruff, affectionate bark, ending sometimes in a howl of sympathy. Donnybrook was also concerned, adding a soft whicker from the nearby paddock. There was real companionship in that back yard.

I did what I could to make the imprisonment more bearable. I always shared at least one meal a day in Rascal's cage, and we were together before and after school. I took him to the garden to help me harvest the dry navy beans and Hubbard squashes. He liked to have me rake leaves, burrowing into each bright pile and popping up to surprise me from unexpected places. And he became a real asset in the new job I had taken selling magazines. He attracted customers wherever we went.

There must be hundreds of thousands of men who sold

the *Saturday Evening Post* when they were boys, and I joined their ranks during the first week of October. I was very short of cash, and I realized that I would have to work harder if I were ever to earn the money for the canvas for my canoe.

Putting Rascal in my bicycle basket, I pedaled down to the magazine and stationery store owned by Frank Ash, which occupied the building next to the Tobacco Exchange Bank. The big bundles of *Posts* had just arrived on the Thursday train, and each of us took fifty copies as a starter. On the cover was a little girl placing a garland of flowers around a service flag. And I was impressed all over again by the fact that this magazine had been founded by Benjamin Franklin.

Either Frank Ash, or the circulation manager of the Curtis Publishing Company, had made a diabolical decision in a desperate attempt to unload another of their periodicals. For each fifty *Posts* we had to sell five copies of the *Country Gentleman*. Ours was a town filled with retired farmers, but not one of them wanted that magazine. Rascal furnished such an animated sideshow, however, that we often persuaded customers to take both publications.

We bicycled through the autumn dusk crying, *"Saturday Evening Post,* five cents. Get your *Post* here, Mister, five cents—only five cents! *Saturday Evening Post?"*

It was rumored that in biology class we were to learn the facts of life that year. Most of us already had some misinformation on the subject, but I was very vague as to how little girls are constructed. However, being not-quite twelve, I was not in complete despair about my ignorance.

What did puzzle me however was how such a lovely, delicate creature as Miss Whalen, with lights in her hair and eyes, could possibly tell a mixed class how babies are made. Fortunately this would come much later in the term, and she would have many months to lead up to the subject by way of the lesser fauna.

Our biology teacher had her own method of inspiring the class. She taught instinctively. If wild geese were noticed crossing the October sky, she would call us all to the windows to hear their distant clangor and to watch them V-ing southward. She told us how one gander after another took that difficult position at the point of the V, breaking the air resistance for those behind, and how these same brave male birds—sometimes a *widowed* gander—kept lonely vigil all night, guarding over the flock while the others slept.

"We are on a branch of the great Mississippi Flyway," she said. "That is why we have the wonderful opportunity of watching so many thousands of birds migrating northward in the spring and south again in the autumn."

Then she told us that wild geese (like swans) are mated for life, and accompany each other, season after season, to rear their goslings in the Arctic and to winter in the southern bayous.

"That is why it is wicked to shoot a wild goose or swan," she said. "It leaves a widowed mate."

On the first day of school she captured our attention by

asking each of us about our pets. Almost everyone had a cat or dog or canary or pony. But I was the only one in the class who had a raccoon. Many animals were to be invited on various days to attend our biology class.

She asked Bud Babcock to bring his little terrier to school, and other pupils to bring goldfish, a parrot, and a tame squirrel. But Rascal and I had the honor of receiving the first such invitation.

After class I stayed for a moment to talk to Miss Whalen about my raccoon, and to ask her a question which had been intriguing me for several weeks.

"Do you think raccoons will become human beings sometime?" I asked hopefully.

"Why, Sterling, what a strange idea."

"Earnest Hooton, who lives next door to us, is studying anthropology. And he has a theory that the *hands* teach the *brain*."

"Yes," Miss Whalen said thoughtfully, "possibly they do."

"And he thinks that because our apelike ancestors stood up and used their hands, and developed simple tools, their brains developed too."

"That's an exciting idea," my teacher said.

"Well, my raccoon uses his hands all the time, and gets brighter every day. So in one hundred million years or so, couldn't raccoons develop into something like human beings?"

"Stranger things have happened," Miss Whalen said. "I'm very eager to see your bright raccoon."

She gave me a warm smile, but she didn't laugh at me

or call my question silly. And I left the classroom feeling that Miss Whalen was a very special person.

On the morning Rascal was invited, I brushed and combed him until his dark guard hairs shone and his gray underfur was as soft as lamb's wool. I used silver polish on his nameplate and saddle soap on his slender collar and leash. After all, it was to be Rascal's first day at school, and I wanted him to make the best possible impression.

Fortunately biology was our first class in the morning, so we didn't have too long to wait.

Rascal's behavior was excellent. Clean, well-groomed, alert, and polite, he sat on Miss Whalen's desk as though he had spent most of his short life addressing biology classes. He asked a few questions about her glass paper-weight (which, when shaken, produced a snowstorm over a toy village); and he gently examined this small globe of glass.

"As you can see," Miss Whalen began, "raccoons are curious."

Then she wrote on the blackboard: *Raccoon*—an Indian word meaning "he who scratches."

Slammy Stillman raised his hand. "Does he scratch because he has fleas?" This produced laughter, and the teacher rapped lightly for order.

I raised my hand and was acknowledged. "Miss Whalen, Rascal is perfectly clean. He goes swimming every day and he never had a flea in his life."

"I think," said the teacher, "the Indians meant that raccoons scratch and dig for turtle eggs and other food along the shore. Sometimes they even dig for earth-worms."

Slammy scowled and slumped deeper in his seat.

"Does this raccoon remind you of any other animal?" Miss Whalen asked.

"He looks like a little bear," Bud Babcock said.

"You are right, Bud," the teacher agreed. "He is a cousin of the bear and is sometimes called a 'wash bear' because he washes all his food as we will show you in a few minutes." She took a piece of chalk and again wrote on the blackboard: *Procyon lotor*—his Latin name. *Lotor* meaning "washer."

I was intrigued because Miss Whalen was telling us certain things that even I didn't know about Rascal. Now she brought out a shallow enameled laboratory pan, which contained not only water, but, to my surprise, a crayfish. This she put before Rascal on her desk.

"Now let's see what the raccoon will do."

Rascal, like the wonderful little ham he always was, looked around the class and off through the windows while running his hands with a kneading motion all over the shallow pan. He knew exactly where the crayfish was, but he was showing off. Suddenly his body stiffened for a pounce, and two seconds later he had his prey fast in his grip and was washing it blissfully in anticipation of his feast.

By this time the class was as happy as Rascal, and almost everybody clapped.

"Raccoons are *omnivorous*," Miss Whalen said, writing the word on the blackboard. "This means they will eat almost anything. They live from the Atlantic to the Pacific and from southern Canada to Mexico. They have from two to six raccoon kits every May—usually in a hollow tree. And these kits mind their mother very well, trundling after her as she teaches them how to fish the edge of the creeks. They are friendly animals unless attacked, but can sometimes kill a dog if backed into a corner."

Miss Whalen asked me if I would tell briefly of my experiences with my raccoon, and I stood before the class, petting Rascal as I talked. I think we had the attention of all but Slammy, particularly when Rascal climbed on my shoulder and started vaguely playing with my ear.

"I even sleep with him sometimes," I confessed. "He's a wonderful pet."

Everyone wanted to touch him after that. So, one by one, my classmates came up and petted him, some of the girls pretending to be a little frightened. Slammy was last of the line and he slouched up, shifty-eyed and sneering. I was watching for trouble, but was a moment too late. Just as he reached the raccoon, Slammy stretched a heavy rubber band and snapped Rascal in the face.

Very rarely before had I heard Rascal emit his scream of rage. But this was pure fury—a fight-to-the-death cry— and in a split second Rascal sank his fine, sharp teeth into Slammy's fat hand.

Slammy yelled until you could have heard him in the assembly hall. He danced around shaking his hand, screaming, "Mad 'coon! Mad 'coon!—you gotta shoot him now—mad 'coon!"

Miss Whalen's voice was cold and severe. "Slammy Stillman, everyone in this room saw what you did. If you think this is a mad raccoon, then you need no other punishment than the worry you will experience wondering if indeed you have rabies. Here, use some of this iodine on your little bite. Class is dismissed. Sterling, will you stay for a moment?"

I didn't know what my teacher would decree, but it proved almost as severe a punishment as she had given Slammy. She said, "I'm sorry, but under the circumstances you will have to cage your raccoon constantly for the next fourteen days. If he should show signs of rabies we would still have time to get Pasteur treatments for Slammy."

"But he isn't rabid," I protested. "You saw what happened."

"I certainly did. And I feel certain he is a perfectly healthy animal. But we can't take a chance."

She was silent for a moment. When she turned back to me her mood had changed and she said quietly, "Rascal is a wonderful pet. Thank you for bringing him to class, and for your good oral report." She petted the raccoon and added, "You'd better take him home to his cage, Sterling. I'll explain to the other teachers why you'll be absent for the rest of the day."

As I pedaled homeward, with Rascal in the bicycle basket, he had already forgotten his recent fight. It was a crisp, clear autumn day as we entered the cage to begin the two-week sentence. I had a crazy, affectionate thought: if they have to lock up Rascal, they'll have to lock me up with him.

We sat eating soft-shelled pecans, wishing we could stay side by side forever, sharing a meal and each other's company.

Slammy, unfortunately, did not die of rabies. In fact the punctures in his hands healed almost immediately. But the punishment inflicted on Rascal and me continued. We were jailmates for as many hours a day as I could join him.

Rascal was beginning to get slightly plump in preparation for the winter. I gave him any food he wanted, so we were not too unhappy in his cage.

On the fourteenth day of his confinement, when he had not shown a single sign of any sickness, I opened the door and we frisked out into the autumn world. We walked up the street to Crescent Drive and turned down the country lane through a world ablaze with autumn. It was Indian summer. The corn shocks, pale as buckskin tepees, pointed upward to the immense blue curve of the sky, and maples flamed along the ridges.

As we passed Bardeen's orchard we helped ourselves to a few apples. Farther down the lane where the fences were garlanded with wild grapes, Rascal dyed his muzzle purple with this pure pigment.

Each autumn it was necessary to examine the hickory and walnut trees we hoped to raid, and to estimate the number of muskrats living in the sloughs and ponds where we hoped to trap. This was a jaunt I usually took with my trapping-and-hickory-nutting partner Oscar Sun-

143

derland. Oscar was not at home, however, so Rascal and I made the survey without him.

On the bank above the swimming hole we came upon the sorrowful sight of a great walnut stump where a giant tree had been standing only a few months before. I had often rested in the shade of that tree, and gathered its nuts in the autumn, staining my hands dark brown with the hulls. Here too I had captured the only Royal Walnut moth in my collection. Now the trunk had been cut for rifle stocks, as had so many walnut trees that season. I found a red "writing stone" in the creek and in big, angry letters printed on the stump: DAMN THE MAN WHO CUT THIS TREE.

Gradually I forgot my anger, however, as we skirted the marshes and ponds to the north. Never before had I seen so many new muskrat houses—those conical piles of reeds, with underwater entrances, which make such perfect homes for these harmless and interesting fur-bearing rodents. I had raised several muskrat kits and turned them loose in other years. I could never bear to kill and skin those I had reared by hand. Rascal and I sat silently beside a marshy pond where a few mallards and black ducks were tipping and preening. As evening began to fall, the muskrats came quietly from their half-finished houses and began to cut cattails, which they carried in their mouths through the still water to pile upon their homes.

We wandered happily back to town through the dusk, the flame of the maples muted in the dying light.

VII: *November*

SPANISH influenza, which had swept across Europe and the eastern states, hit Brailsford Junction late in October, killing more of our citizens than died in the war. The schools were closed, and people scurried along the half-deserted streets wearing eerie-looking masks of white gauze. At least one person in four was dangerously ill, with twice that number less seriously affected. Sometimes the disease struck with swift fatality. One ancient couple on the northern edge of town struggled out to their well to get a pail of water. The old man died at the pump, and his wife collapsed beside him, the handle of the bucket still grasped in her stiffening fingers.

Mine was one of the milder cases. But on this occasion my father seemed concerned. He bundled me in several sweaters and blankets and helped me into the car. I begged to take Rascal with me, and he consented.

We drove slowly through the increasingly leafless countryside toward the old North homestead, now operated by my father's brother Fred and his gentle wife Lillian. I was to be placed in the care of Aunt Lillie, who never refused a sick child or an orphaned lamb. It had not occurred to my father to telephone her. He, like Uncle Fred, merely took her for granted.

She had been an attractive young schoolteacher when my Uncle Fred had come courting in the 1890's in a dashing rig behind a prancing team, and she still had traces of her former beauty after bearing three sons, cooking, washing, cleaning, and mending, gathering eggs and churning butter throughout these many years. She said that when she died she wanted to come back to the farm and do it all over again, because this was her idea of heaven.

My Uncle Fred was of a coarser grain—but Aunt Lillie loved him. Rough, sun-browned, and strong, and weighing a well-proportioned two hundred pounds, his jocosity was tinged with cruelty. He delighted in teasing Aunt Lillie by playing, on his Edison talking machine, a cylinder record entitled, "Why I Picked a Lemon in the Garden of Love Where They Say Only Peaches Grow."

Aunt Lillie would sigh a trifle sadly and go on with her ceaseless labor while my uncle chuckled, immensely pleased with himself and his wit.

However, no one worked harder or longer hours than my Uncle Fred. With fifty-two cows to milk by hand, two hundred hogs to feed, forty acres of tobacco to set, hoe, cultivate, top, sucker, harvest, strip, and bundle, and one hundred and twenty additional acres of hay, corn, and oats to plant and harvest, there were not enough daylight hours during the summer to do the work. Uncle Fred drove his three teen-age sons as hard as he drove himself. And if he ever gave it a thought, he must have felt that his wife's work was easier than his own.

His hobbies at various times included photography and taxidermy, the raising of canaries and goldfish in commercial quantities, the breeding of Merino sheep, Shetland ponies, ferrets, Belgian hares, and fancy pigeons. He bought and repaired threshing machines. And he loved nothing so much as butchering day (an agony to uncomplaining Aunt Lillie, as lambs she had bottle-fed, calves and pigs she had nursed, went to the knife).

Somehow, despite all this, it was a happy marriage, and the great old farmhouse offered a warm rural welcome.

Aunt Lillie came out to greet us, wiping her hands on her apron in that perpetual gesture of humbleness which seemed to afflict whole generations of farm wives, who gave so much to so many in return for so little.

"Oh my, it's Willard and Sterling! Why, Sterling, are you sick?"

"Just a touch of influenza, Lillian," my father said. "I thought that perhaps . . ."

"Why of course, Willard. He needs my care. We'll put him up in the bedroom next to ours, off the parlor. It won't be a bit of trouble. Come in for a cup of coffee and a second breakfast."

We went into the pleasant, fragrant kitchen with its

147

great range dominating the middle of the room, its long table always spread with a clean gingham cloth, plants blooming at the windows, rifles and shotguns stacked in a corner.

From the range she brought the huge graniteware coffeepot and poured steaming coffee into thick ironware cups.

"Now I can fix you ham and eggs or bacon and eggs in just a moment," Aunt Lillie said, "and toast of course. It isn't store bread—just some I baked."

I looked up at my father hoping he would say something adequate, but he didn't. So I tried to be gracious.

"Your bread is the best I ever ate," I said. "And we don't need ham and eggs, Aunt Lillie . . . and thank you for everything."

"Why bless you," Aunt Lillie said happily, "you're always welcome—you and your little raccoon too. You're like a fourth son to me, Sterling."

I think that for just a moment my father was aware of the imposition upon Aunt Lillie, perhaps even remembering my mother and how she bore all four of us—Theo, Jessica, Herschel, and myself—while he was conveniently absent. But all he said was, "Just toast and coffee, Lillian. I hope Sterling won't be a burden for a couple of weeks."

"I know Fred will be sorry to miss you," Aunt Lillie said, bringing the toast and preserves. "He and Charles are shooting squirrels down on the old Kumlien place. Wilfred is repairing a threshing machine and Ernest is upstairs studying his schoolbooks. He'll be down in a little while."

I sipped the good coffee, munched the wonderful toast, and thought that in this world there must be few such human beings as Aunt Lillie.

For several days I spent most of my time in bed, arising occasionally for tea and toast or a short walk with Rascal. In the evening, however, I donned bathrobe and slippers to listen to Aunt Lillie reading to the family in the parlor. The big base-burner with its glowing coals sent ruddy light toward the dim corners where well-worn, red velvet chairs and couches and an ornate parlor organ lent touches of faded elegance.

Aunt Lillie sat in her rocker beside a small table where a kerosene lamp threw its pale radiance upon the pages of a farm magazine. We sprawled around her in comfort, listening to her gentle voice as she read an endless serial.

Rascal had absolutely no interest in this story, but he was fascinated by the jungle of beasts and birds inhabiting this room. Safely above the floor level, cardinals, scarlet tanagers, indigo buntings, and two of the last passenger pigeons ever seen in Wisconsin perched in perpetual silence on varnished branches amid wax foliage and flowers.

Grouped on the floor, eyes gleaming with reflected light, were many four-footed creatures Uncle Fred had shot, skinned, and stuffed in lifelike poses. Badgers and woodchucks, a fox kit and a ferocious timber wolf made one unlikely grouping under the curve of the stairway. Rascal moved among potential enemies, alert and cautious. He

149

was particularly intrigued by a mother raccoon and her offspring, arranged on the bole of a wild cherry tree.

During a pause between chapters of the story, my uncle observed that raccoons are very interesting animals. "Mighty good eating too. Looks like you're fattening Rascal to make a 'coon dinner."

"Now, Fred," Aunt Lillie admonished mildly, "Sterling loves his little raccoon."

"Who taught you how to stuff animals, Uncle Fred?" I asked, hoping to change the subject.

"Thure Kumlien," my uncle said, a note of respect in his voice. "A great old fellow, Kumlien. Knew taxidermy from A to Z. Only trouble was, he'd draw a bead on a bird he wanted and then lower his gun—too tender-hearted."

"He was fond of birds," Aunt Lillie said. "He couldn't bear to kill them."

"I could kill birds all day," my uncle said. "Used to shoot down passenger pigeons by the bushel basket."

"And they're all gone now," Aunt Lillie reminded him. "Not one passenger pigeon left in North America."

"Let's get on with the story, Lillian."

Contrite for having been so bold, Aunt Lillie began again in her tired voice, column after column of small print, hard to decipher by lamplight. Outside, an autumn wind was slowly rising, moaning at the corners of the house. One by one, Charlie, Wilfred, and Ernest had fallen asleep—and finally Uncle Fred. Rascal had come to curl in my lap. Aunt Lillie's voice faltered and then was still.

The coals in the base-burner glowed less brightly now, and the eyes of the silent animals, watching from the shadows, dimmed in the outer gloom. The kerosene lamp still shed its pool of light over Aunt Lillie's graceful head. In a moment now we would be off to our beds—Rascal's and mine, warm and inviting; my cousins' less so in the frigid rooms above.

Another November night had dropped its curtain on southern Wisconsin.

On the fifth morning of my visit, Rascal and I joined the family at four A.M. for "first breakfast." Aunt Lillie, of course, had been the earliest to arise, building a fire in the kitchen range with dry wood which Ernest had ready for her in the wood box.

Uncle Fred arose next. His method of waking his sons was to strip back all the covers in those freezing rooms, shouting jovially, "Milking time. Rise and shine."

We gathered in the kitchen for a "light" meal of ham and eggs, hot muffins, and coffee served by lamplight which gleamed upon the black windows. Charles, oldest of the boys, was always a little sullen in the morning. But he roused himself enough to tickle Rascal's belly, trying to make him fight.

Wilfred was soft-spoken and gracious. He fed my raccoon bits of ham from his own plate and promised to give him a fast ride on his motorcycle.

Ernest performed a strange service for any male in that household. He helped his mother put breakfast on the table, and suggested that she sit down to eat with the rest of us. Aunt Lillie gave him a grateful look, but said she would eat later.

While we consumed her country breakfast, my aunt busied herself lighting the lanterns we would need. Among her many chores was the daily task of keeping the lamps and lanterns brightly polished and filled with kerosene.

Her four "menfolks" arose without a word of thanks, put on old hunting caps, plaid jackets, and cowhide boots. Each took a lantern and a shining milk pail.

I was as warmly bundled as the others as we plunged into the outer darkness, lowering our heads to fight the blustering wind. My uncle led the line. Rascal and I brought up the rear. The swinging lanterns hollowed out the dark, throwing our shadows grotesquely against the barn and straw stack which loomed, mountainous and forbidding, just ahead.

Inside the barn we were swallowed by a beamed cavern, inhabited by rows upon rows of drowsy animals. These stables were well cleaned and freshly limed each day. They had an odor that will always be nostalgic to me— faintly acrid of course, but mingled too with the fragrance of clover hay, the sour tang of silage, the astringent dust of lime, and the warm, good smell of the cows themselves.

Hanging their lanterns on convenient pegs, my uncle and my cousins took hay forks and distributed the morning feeding to the cows. Then, sitting on three-legged milk stools, with their milk pails firmly clasped between their knees, they began sending rhythmic and ringing streams of milk into the buckets. It is a soul-satisfying sound, soothing to cows and milkers. The bells soften and the music deepens as the pail fills.

Again it was fortunate that I had Rascal on his leash, for as we walked the feed lane ahead of the animals, a few old cows were cantankerous, hooking their horns and bellowing at him.

The barn cats too were a trifle suspicious. But when Rascal learned their trick, sitting up just as they did and opening his mouth to get his share of the milk being squirted their way, they accepted him as a veritable equal.

Each milker had thirteen cows to milk—a long, long process. Rascal and I soon went to sleep on a pile of fresh hay beneath the hay chute. When we awoke it was to the cheerful boom of Uncle Fred's voice: "Come on, boy! Come on, 'coon! Milking's done. Time for second breakfast."

As I grew stronger I helped with all the minor chores such as gathering eggs, feeding the calves, and swilling the pigs. The autumn litters were becoming plump, vociferous porkers with greedy appetites.

Under a huge iron kettle near the pig yard, Ernest and I built a crackling fire. Into the kettle we dumped forty or fifty gallons of fresh buttermilk to which we added ground feed, stirring the supplement into the liquid as it heated. When the mixture became warm we dipped it out, pouring it into long feed troughs. This produced such a wild scramble among the squealing, struggling, slurping beasts that Rascal climbed a nearby apple tree and refused to come down until the pigs had cleaned the troughs and were grunting drowsily in satiated contentment.

Rascal liked the lambs, the big work horses, and most of the other animals. But he never did learn to love pigs.

My small part of the farm duties left me with plenty of time for pure pleasure. With Rascal on his leash, we visited the haylofts, filled almost to the eaves with clover and alfalfa hay. Here there were always sounds of pigeons cooing, sparrows bickering, and mice rustling—such somnolent music that we sometimes fell asleep, cupped in a hollow in the hay, safe from the wind and cold.

The grain bins, filled with wheat and oats, invited a dangerous leap into deep waters. But since on one occasion I had barely been rescued from smothering in wheat, I now restrained my raccoon, who was unaware of his danger.

In the tobacco sheds the leaves were brittle and brown. They held no fascination for Rascal, who preferred the hams and sides of bacon hanging in the smokehouse, the cream and fresh-churned butter in the spring house, and particularly the top delight of the entire farm (as far as this little bear was concerned), the honey in the honey house.

It was Aunt Lillie who thought of this special treat. She put on an old gray sweater, neatly mended at the elbows, threw a shawl over her head, and led us through the bee yard to the little brick building where honey was extracted. Inside this efficient room was a big metal drum containing revolving racks which threw the honey from the combs by centrifugal force.

The extractor was not in operation at the moment, but enough liquid honey was in the bottom of the drum to fill several Mason jars. It ran slowly because of the low temperature. However, the golden stream filled one jar after another as we waited—the net result of tens of thousands of journeys by the bees bringing nectar from clover fields all over the countryside.

"Now it's time for you and Rascal to have *your* honey," Aunt Lillie said, handing me a clean spoon.

Rascal and I shared the spoon, of course, having been messmates on many another occasion. But I didn't get my share of the honey because Rascal had found his favorite delicacy since sweet corn. Aunt Lillie did not laugh very often, but she was laughing now until she had to wipe her eyes on a corner of her apron. The wildly excited raccoon had found the dripping honey faucet, and was upside down, doing his best to get every drop left in the drum.

"Oh, Sterling, what a charming little animal." She put an arm around me as we watched, and I suddenly had an overwhelming desire to tell her how much she meant to me.

I think she knew without words, because when I looked up she was not laughing, only smiling tenderly. We took the Mason jars of honey and, leading the very reluctant raccoon, headed back to the farmhouse through the bright and frosty morning.

False Armistice Day and my twelfth birthday fell on the same date. Aunt Lillie answered three long rings on the party line, which meant a general message for all phones.

It was during second breakfast, and we were at the table. Even before she hung up the receiver she was saying. "Oh how wonderful! Oh thank our Heavenly Father! It's over, it's all over. They've stopped all that terrible killing in France."

"You mean the war's really over, Lillian?" Uncle Fred asked.

"All over. They're signing an armistice."

I couldn't have asked for a better birthday present than this (even if everyone *had* forgotten it was my birthday). I wanted to be alone to think about it. And so I went with Rascal to the pony stable and we sat for a time on a bale of straw looking at Nellie, her mate Teddy, and their twin colts Pansy and Pancho Villa.

So the war was actually over at last, and that nightmare had come to an end. Herschel would return from France, and we could go fishing together.

The realization came slowly, then with a rush, and I was jubilantly happy. I picked up my raccoon and danced him around, while he cocked his head and chirred a question.

"Let's have a pony ride, Rascal."

Of all these ponies, Teddy was my favorite, a little black devil of a stallion with more tricks than a trained seal. No one had taught him these wicked, joyous quirks and eccentricities. They were built into his nature along with the winds and storms of the Shetland Islands—a throwback to some wild ancestor centuries before his time.

157

He nipped the flanks of cows when we were driving them home from pasture. He backed into tethered teams, kicking and squealing until he sometimes started a runaway. He was a veritable bucking bronco on occasion, rearing and whinnying his defiance to the whole world. He had a very tough mouth (and none of these pony bridles had a curb).

I had learned to ride him, however, and was seldom thrown unless he resorted to his mischievous trick of running under certain limbs of trees which he knew were high enough to clear him, but not to clear the rider. It was always a contest with Teddy, and you could gain his respect only by winning, whereupon he would reward you with a smooth, fast ride—his mane streaming in the wind.

However Teddy was demonstrating at this very moment that he didn't like Rascal, and I wasn't risking the life of my raccoon on such a violent mount. The twin colts were far too young to ride, and of course were untrained. This left only Nellie, a broad and comfortable little mare who was as tolerant of Teddy as my Aunt Lillie was of Uncle Fred.

Nellie took us aboard with no fuss whatsoever, as though she had spent her life carrying the double load of a boy and his raccoon. Rascal sat ahead of me as he had on the wooden ponies of the merry-go-round. We trotted down the lane to the pasture, passing still pools where spearpoints of ice extended over the black depths, and groves of hickory trees where I had already gathered more than a bushel of nuts. We came at last to the solitude of Kumlien's woods and ambled along its winding paths.

There could be no better place to contemplate peace on earth than in this forest where the old naturalist had lived his quiet life.

That evening Aunt Lillie cooked a very special feast, not because it was my birthday, not even because of the rumored armistice, but because my father was driving out for dinner, after which he was taking me home. There was roast turkey with hickory-nut dressing, a special recipe of her own. There were mashed potatoes and sweet potatoes and baked Hubbard squash and more relishes and preserves than I can now remember. Finally we had a choice of cold pumpkin pie with whipped cream or hot mince pie, fresh from the oven.

It didn't seem to matter now that everyone had forgotten my birthday. But, of course, it was Aunt Lillie who thought of it. "Why, Sterling," she said remorsefully, putting her hand to her mouth, "it's your twelfth birthday, and not one of us remembered. And I didn't even bake a cake."

Then everybody sang "Happy Birthday" and I felt well rewarded.

My father didn't apologize, but he reached in his pocket and brought forth his own personal watch with its chain finely braided from my mother's chestnut hair.

For several generations that old watch has passed from father to son. (And may the tradition long continue.)

On the morning of November 11, 1918, the real Armistice was signed in a railroad car in France. Although men were killed up to the final hour, the cease-fire came at last and a sudden silence fell over the batteries and trenches and graveyards of Europe. The world was now "safe for democracy." Tyranny had been vanquished forever. The "war to end war" had been won, and there would never be another conflict. Or so we believed in that far-off and innocent time.

In Brailsford Junction the celebration began early. The decorated fire engines, automobiles, and horse-drawn conveyances crowded the streets in a noisy, happy parade. I interwove the spokes of my bicycle wheels with red, white, and blue crepe-paper ribbons. With Rascal in the basket, I pedaled through the throng, ringing my bell as a small contribution to the joyous pandemonium. At eleven o'clock the fire whistle and all the church and schoolbells in town joined the chorus.

During the afternoon my elation slowly subsided, and I began oiling my muskrat traps for the season ahead. Rascal was always interested in whatever I was doing. But when he came to sniff and feel the traps, a terrible thought slowed my fingers. Putting my traps aside I opened one of the catalogues sent to trappers by the St. Louis fur buyers. There, in full color, on the very first page was a handsome raccoon, his paw caught in a powerful trap.

How could anyone mutilate the sensitive, questing hands of an animal like Rascal? I picked up my raccoon and hugged him in a passion of remorse.

I burned my fur catalogues in the furnace and hung my traps in the loft of the barn, never to use them again.

Men had stopped killing other men in France that day; and on that day I signed a permanent peace treaty with the animals and the birds. It is perhaps the only peace treaty that was ever kept.

VIII: *December January February*

THE first flurry of snow came early in December, whirl-
ing a few flakes into Rascal's hollow in the tree. I feared
that a real blizzard might make that den quite uncomfortable. From a piece of sheet copper I fashioned a hood
over the entrance, and I lined the hole itself with old
blankets and an outgrown sweater of mine so that my raccoon would have a snug winter nest. Rascal took an immediate fancy to the sweater, perhaps associating it with
me.

As cold weather set in, Rascal grew sleepy. Raccoons
do not actually hibernate, but they do sleep for many days
at a time, emerging only occasionally to pad around in
the snow seeking a full meal. Every morning before I left
for school I would go into the cage and reach into the
hole. I wanted to make sure that Rascal was safe and
comfortable. It was a great satisfaction to feel his warm,

furry body breathing slowly and rhythmically, and to know that he was sleeping soundly in his pleasant home.

Sometimes he stirred when I petted him, and murmured in his sleep. Now and then he awoke sufficiently to poke his little black-masked face out of the hole to look at me. I always rewarded him with a handful of pecans.

I realized, of course, that our partial separation was only temporary. Many living things sleep through the winter: my woodchucks under the barn, frogs deep in the mud, seeds in their pods, and butterflies in their cocoons. They were merely resting for spring and would awake again with a great burst of new life. Rascal and I would have wonderful times together when the warm months returned.

So with a final pat or two I would tell my pet to go on sleeping. And Rascal, drowsy-eyed, would curl into a ball and return to his winter slumbers.

My financial problems increased as we approached Christmas. In recent autumns I had earned as much as seventy-five dollars trapping muskrats. This allowed me to purchase thoughtful gifts for the family. But since signing my peace treaty with the muskrats and other wild animals, I was finding that peace does not always bring prosperity.

I solicited nearby neighbors and shoveled many walks, earning a top price of fifty cents for moving a couple of tons of snow. I also increased my efforts to sell more *Saturday Evening Posts*. But the silver accumulated very slowly, and prices were frightfully high in the stores. A handsomely illustrated fishing book which I wanted to buy for Herschel was marked five dollars, and fur-lined gloves for my father would be nearly as expensive. Then there were gifts to be purchased for my two sisters, and small things for my pets. At this rate I would never be able to save enough to buy the canvas for my canoe.

One Saturday, after a discouraging tour of the stores, I stopped at the post office to find two cheerful letters in our box. One was the first from Herschel since the Armistice. The other was from my beloved sister Jessica, still taking postgraduate work at the University of Chicago. Both letters relieved my mind in a number of ways.

Herschel had survived the war and influenza. He said the Paris garters I had sent were better than a rabbit's foot. No metal *had* touched him.

War censorship had been lifted, and for the first time my brother was able to tell us where his outfit had been fighting. His single paragraph, listing some of the bloodiest battles of the war, was so quietly factual that it might have been the report of a pleasure tour:

"We spent a couple of months in the Haute-Marne region and then went to the Alsace Sector. Later we joined the Château-Thierry Offensive, the Oise-Aisne Offensive and the Meuse-Argonne. We were on the Meuse at the time of the Armistice."

Then came the disappointing news that he had been ordered to march to the Rhine to help establish a bridgehead near Coblenz, Germany, and that he would not be demobilized for six months at the earliest. He asked us not to send gifts, saying he would bring his presents with him when he came home.

My first reaction was sadness that Herschel would not be with us at Christmas. I had heard nothing concerning an Army of Occupation and had not realized that demobilization is such a slow process. But at least he was alive and unwounded, and I would have a few more months to scrape together the money for the fishing book.

Letters from Jessica were always a joy. Bright, salty, and affectionate, they told so much concerning her unselfish character. Flashes of temper were to be expected. But these were outweighed by the gaiety and Spartan good humor of this sister who had cared for my father and myself for so many months after my mother died.

Jessica was coming home for Christmas. She enclosed a ten-dollar check, made out in my name, to help me with my Christmas shopping. I was very fortunate to have a brother like Herschel and two such sisters as Theo and Jessica.

With my financial crisis eased, I turned to the pleasant tasks of buying a tree and sweeping and decorating the house. My father paid little attention to such matters, and furthermore he was again away on business.

Almost immediately I realized that Rascal presented a new and difficult problem. It had always been our custom to invite some of the animals to be with us on Christmas Eve when we distributed the gifts. In the past we usually had limited the four-footed delegation to Wowser and the best behaved of the cats. But it was unthinkable to exclude Rascal, who, however, could never discipline his hands when shining objects were within his reach.

He could examine a glass paperweight or lift the lid of the sugar bowl without breaking glass or crockery. But I could well imagine the damage he might do to the fragile glass balls and figurines on the Christmas tree.

How could we have both Rascal and a Christmas tree? And yet we must have both. The answer to this dilemma struck me as a real inspiration.

There was a large semicircular bay extending from the living room, with six windows that overlooked the flower garden. This was where we always mounted our Christmas tree. I bought and decorated a thick spruce, which tapered gracefully to the star at its tip and nearly filled the bay with its fragrant greenery. This took me most of one Saturday. Then I made careful measurements of the rectangular opening leading to the bay and hastened to my work bench in the barn. I had sufficient chicken wire left from building the cage to cover a frame, designed carefully and precisely to fit the opening I had just measured. In less than an hour I was maneuvering this construction through the big, double front door into the living room. The lumber was white and new, the chicken wire shining. But for a few moments I hesitated before nailing it to the unmarred woodwork of our respectable old house. Still, it required but one nail at each corner of the frame, and I could fill the holes later with putty or wood-filler. Another few minutes and the job was complete. And there, safe behind the wire, was the decorated tree, every bauble secure from my raccoon.

I put a Christmas wreath above the fireplace, laced Christmas ribbons through the ribs of my canoe frame, hung a few sprigs of holly from archways and chandeliers, and stood back to admire the total effect. I was immoderately pleased with my work and could scarcely wait to show it to my father and to Jessica.

When my father returned from his trip, I led him happily into the living room and pointed to the Christmas tree, wired off from the rest of the world as though it might try to escape to its native forest.

"My word," my father said mildly. "What are you building, Sterling, another cage for Rascal?"

"You're warm," I said. "It's so that Rascal can't climb the tree and spoil the ornaments."

"Well," my father hesitated, "at least it's unusual."

"Do you think Jessica will hit the ceiling?"

"She might," my father said. "You never can tell what Jessica might do."

There was one train a day from Chicago, an old ten-wheeler pulling a baggage car, a passenger coach, and sometimes a freight car and a caboose. We loved that train and listened for it to rumble across the river bridge, blow four times for the lower crossing, and come huffing and puffing up the slight grade to the station. My late grandfather had often spoken of the first train that had ever rolled over these tracks, with twenty yoke of oxen helping it up the grade. But ours was a better and much newer engine.

There seemed to be a special music to the bell of our ten-wheeler, and a special corona made by its exhaust steam as it pulled to a halt and hissed its hot vapor into

167

the sunlight. Train time was exciting even if the passenger coach did not carry someone as much loved as my sister Jessica.

The conductor helped her down the steps and my father and I took her suitcase and her many packages. She was wearing a wide-brimmed velvet hat which looked very fashionable, a new coat with a fur collar, and high-laced shoes that came to the hem of her dress. She had recently sold several groups of poems and a short story, and she seemed quite affluent.

"Merry Christmas, Jessica. Welcome home," we cried.

She kissed us, and then held me off and looked at me critically. "You've outgrown your Mackinaw, Sterling. And you'll catch your death of cold not wearing a cap."

"He never wears a cap," my father explained.

Obviously I was clean, and had combed my stubborn curls into some semblance of order, so Jessica wasn't altogether disapproving.

We went homeward through the iron-cold air and bright sunlight, up Fulton Street, past all the stores. We turned right on Albion, past the Carnegie Public Library and the Methodist Church, then left on Rollin Street, and there we were, still laughing and chattering and asking a hundred questions in the manner of most families gathering for Christmas.

Perhaps we were extra gay to cover an underlying sadness. Mother would not be at the gracious double door to greet us. Herschel was still in France, but "alive and un-wounded" as we kept repeating. Theo and her kind husband Norman would be spending Christmas in their own home far to the north. Already our closely knit family was dwindling and dispersing as all families eventually must. But the three of us would do the best we could to bring cheer to the old house.

As we entered the living room, I wasn't sure whether Jessica wanted to laugh or cry. I had done my best in decorating the tree and the canoe, which was supposed to hold our cargo of gifts. But suddenly I saw it through my sister's eyes—an unfinished boat, chicken wire, and dust on the furniture.

"You simply *can't* go on living like this!" she said. "You *must* hire a full-time housekeeper."

"But, Dottie," I pleaded, using her pet name, "I worked so hard on the tree and decorations, and the cage to keep Rascal out."

Then Jessica was laughing and hugging me in the crazy way she often acted (much the way I acted, too). She was, and is, the most spontaneously affectionate, thoughtful, brilliant, and unreasonable sister one could wish for. A very attractive combination, I have always maintained.

"At least we can take the canoe to the barn," Jessica said (not wishing to lose her advantage).

"But, Dottie, I can't take it to the barn. It's cold as blazes out there. I have to put on the canvas first."

"Well, put on the canvas, and we'll still have time to clean this room for Christmas."

"That sounds sensible," my father agreed.

"But you don't understand," I explained. "I had to spend all my money to build the cage, and then all the other money I could scrape together to buy Christmas presents, and . . ."

"Sterling, get to the point," Jessica said.

"So I haven't any money left for canvas, and it will cost about fifteen dollars, I think."

Jessica looked at my father severely, and he said, "Now be reasonable, Jessica. I'm a busy man. I can't know everything that's going on in Sterling's head and I didn't know he needed money for canvas."

Jessica sighed, realizing that we were both quite hopeless and greatly in need of her care. "Well, at least I can cook you some decent meals and clean up this house."

"It's perfectly clean," I protested. "I swept every single room and shook out the throw rugs and scoured the bathrooms. You don't know how hard I worked getting this place beautiful for you. And, besides, we like our own cooking, and we don't want a housekeeper. You sound like Theo."

"We're happy," my father said. "As happy as we can be since your mother died."

"Don't be sentimental," Jessica said fiercely, wiping tears from her own eyes. "You just wait until I get on an apron! And another thing, you're going to have a housekeeper whether you like it or not."

On the day before Christmas we wrapped our gifts in secrecy in various rooms of the house, camouflaging some in odd-sized packages. We arranged them according to the recipient: those for my father in the prow of the canoe, those for Jessica in the stern, and those for me amidships.

After an early dinner we brought in the animals—Rascal first, to allow him to wake up for the festivities, then Wowser, and finally the selected cats. Jessica immediately fell in love with my raccoon. And when she saw how he struggled to reach through the wire to touch the Christmas-tree baubles, she forgave me for building the barricade.

The Yule log was blazing in the fireplace, shedding light on the tree and its ornaments and making the chicken wire gleam like a dew-drenched cobweb. The argosy of brightly wrapped gifts greatly intrigued my raccoon.

Animals, like children, find it difficult to wait for a gift which is almost within reach. So we always gave them their presents first. Each cat received a catnip mouse, making the old toms and tabbies as playful as kittens, and causing a certain amount of possessive growling. For Wowser, confined to his bath towel on the hearth, I had a new collar which Garth Shadwick had fashioned. But for my pampered pet, Rascal, I had only Christmas candies and pecans, being unable to think of a single other thing he might need.

In opening the family packages we proceeded in rotation. This gave us a chance to admire each object and to express gratitude. There were many thoughtfully chosen books, ties, socks, warm gloves, scarves—all appreciated.

The best gifts came last. Theo and Norman had been quite extravagant. They had sent Jessica a fur muff and my father a sheared beaver cap. To me they had given shoe ice skates, very rare in our region in those days. I eagerly awaited our next game of hockey.

My father brought forth from his pocket a small buckskin pouch and poured into his hand seven beautifully cut and polished agates. They were ringed like Rascal's tail, from golden yellow through oak-leaf brown to deep maroon. With unexpected forethought he had sent our best rough stones from Lake Superior to a gem-cutting firm in Chicago, insisting that they be returned in time for Christmas.

My father was pleased by our response. He chose three agates for Jessica and three for me. Then he did a most surprising thing. Calling for Rascal, he handed him the handsome little stone that the raccoon himself had found.

Always fascinated by shining objects, Rascal felt it carefully, sat up, holding it between his hands to examine it and smell it, then carried it to the corner where he kept his pennies and unceremoniously dropped it among his other treasures. He came back chirring cheerfully.

This might well have topped the gift-giving. But one more large package still lay amidships, "To Sterling, from Jessica." I was very curious but could not imagine what it might be. Upon removing the wrappings I found an unbelievable present—enough heavy, strong white canvas to cover my entire canoe. I was near to unwanted tears, but Jessica saved the day.

"Now perhaps we can get this canoe out of the living room," she said.

Wowser, Rascal, and the cats were soon asleep around us. My father asked Jessica to read from the second chapter of St. Luke, as Mother had done on so many Christmas Eves.

"And it came to pass in those days, that there went out a decree from Caesar Augustus . . .

"And she brought forth her firstborn son, and wrapped him in swaddling clothes, and laid him in a manger; because there was no room for them in the inn . . .

"And there were in the same country, shepherds, abiding in the field, keeping watch over their flock by night . . .

"And, lo, the angel of the Lord came upon them . . . and they were sore afraid."

Faintly through the drifting snow came the strains of the church organ playing "Silent Night, Holy Night."

We put out all the pets except my raccoon—the cats to curl in the hay of the barn, Wowser to sleep in his double-walled doghouse on his blankets. But Rascal went to bed with me. As we dropped off to sleep I wondered if at midnight raccoons speak as other animals are said to do.

It is good to remember that I was given those swift and shining skates early enough in my life so that I could use them for three happy winters. By the fourth winter I was in a wheel chair. And even when I learned to walk, I was never able to skate again.

At twelve, however, I could skate all day, play hockey for hours, and cut simple figures on the ice. It is the nearest thing to flying which man has achieved. Or so it seems in memory.

I had taught Rascal to be a living coonskin hat. He would take a firm grip on my ruck of curly hair, brace his strong hind paws on the collar of my Mackinaw, and enjoy the wildest rides he had ever experienced as we glided forward and backward over Culton's ice pond just south of the railroad tracks.

Slammy Stillman, who had weak ankles as well as a weak brain, came to Culton's pond one day, clamped on his skates, and came wobbling into the gay throng. Rascal and I saw a chance for well-deserved revenge. Without so much as touching the town bully we rushed him and turned on a dime, throwing shaved ice in his unhandsome face.

He went down screaming, "Mad 'coon! Mad 'coon! I'll teach you a lesson."

But the jeering laughter of fifty boys and girls must still be ringing in his ears. He never gave either of us another moment of trouble.

The wall telephone in the living room rang insistently through the echoing reaches of our house at two A.M. on a foggy morning in February. I leaped from bed to answer. The voice that came booming over the wire was that of my Uncle Fred.

"Is your father there?"

"He's asleep upstairs."

"Well, wake him up, Sterling. It's case weather."

"Case weather," I shouted with excitement. "I'll wake

him. And we'll be out there in less than an hour if we can start the Oldsmobile."

"OK, son."

"May I bring Rascal?"

There was a good-natured chuckle at the other end. "Sure, fetch him along. We need all the extra hands we can rally."

"*Case weather*, Daddy," I shouted up the curving stairway. "Uncle Fred needs us right away."

I lit a fire in the kitchen stove, prepared a pot of coffee and a skillet of eggs, and hurried to wake Rascal. He came to the kitchen blinking like a sleepy owl.

It certainly was case weather—fog so thick you could cut it with a knife. By the time we had eaten, started the car, and driven beyond the street lights of the town, we wondered if we would be able to follow the icy ruts.

Lamplight glimmered from the windows of almost every farmhouse. Lanterns, enhaloed by the fog, bobbed along the paths leading to the tobacco sheds.

Case weather—usually a sudden February thaw—softened the tobacco leaves, making it possible to handle them without damage. The warm, moist atmosphere might blanket the region for only a few hours or for several days. During that unpredictable interval, every lath loaded with tobacco plants must be taken from the drying sheds and piled in the stripping house, there to be covered with canvas to keep the moist leaves from freezing. It was back-breaking labor at breakneck speed, but filled with a desperate sort of excitement—a sporting event on which each tobacco farmer was betting his whole year's crop.

We expected Uncle Fred to call us at any time of the day or night when case weather began. And the number of automobiles and buggies groping their way through the fog showed that many others from Brailsford Junction were on a similar mission.

The chains were on the car all winter, and we were very grateful for the added traction as we slithered through slush and mud. But we safely reached the old homestead at last.

Without stopping at the lamplighted kitchen where Aunt Lillie was undoubtedly preparing an early feast, we hurried to the largest tobacco shed where Uncle Fred and my three cousins were already high among the beams handing down the pungent, pliable tobacco. Rascal and I scrambled swiftly to the rafters to take our place in that human elevator. The raccoon was slightly bewildered by this new game. But he loved excitement and was content to perch nearby, his eyes green-gold in the lantern light. He must have thought we were slightly insane in a harmless sort of way.

I worked hard and fast on those high beams for nearly an hour, but I was no match for my father, and certainly unable to compete with Uncle Fred and his three husky boys. True, the laths of tobacco plants were not as heavy as they had been during the harvesting, but they were heavy enough as I balanced among the rafters. Trying to maintain my equilibrium, I let one lath of tobacco slip. It fell thirty feet to the floor, missing by inches the men below me. This was my first intimation that I was becoming tired; and my father said quietly, "Sterling, you'd better take your raccoon and go in to see Aunt Lillie."

I felt ashamed to have dropped the tobacco, and to have proved again that I was not fully capable of doing a grown man's work. But to drop another lath might mean an injury to someone below. So, taking Rascal and one of the lanterns, I made my way up the slope to the kitchen door.

Aunt Lillie hugged me, stroked the raccoon, and said, "We shouldn't have called you at two in the morning. . . . Come have some coffee and hot muffins."

"I love case weather," I said, "and your muffins are wonderful." I gave a bite to Rascal, who immediately begged for more.

"I'm glad you came in to visit with me, Sterling. How are my menfolks doing?"

"We've taken down four tiers at one end," I said. "Maybe a quarter of the crop . . . but I dropped a lath, Aunt Lillie."

"Well, you're just a little boy," Aunt Lillie said.

"I'm not a little boy any more," I protested. "I'm twelve years old, and I weigh nearly one hundred pounds. With Rascal on my shoulder I weigh one hundred and eleven."

"You're both growing up," Aunt Lillie said sadly. "I don't like to see things change—children growing up, their parents growing old."

"You're not old, Aunt Lillie."

"I'm forty-seven."

178

"That was the age of my mother," I said. "Will she be forty-seven forever, Aunt Lillie?"

Aunt Lillie failed to answer for a moment, and then she asked me if I wouldn't like more muffins and coffee. We sat quietly for a time, each thinking his own thoughts.

"Well, Sterling," Aunt Lillie said finally, "I suppose you'll eventually be going to college, to learn a profession and to make something of yourself."

"We take it for granted—going to college."

"Your Uncle Fred will never send our boys—or even let them earn their way through school."

There was no bitterness in her voice. She stated this tragedy as a matter of fact that could not be altered. I understood the situation more completely than she realized. Uncle Fred was the only uncle on either side of my family who had left college before graduation. I had heard him say that he didn't want any of his boys to get the superior notion that they knew more than he did.

Aunt Lillie undoubtedly thought life on the old farm was heaven. But I was beginning to see lines of worry on her face.

"Now what profession have you chosen?"

"I haven't thought about it very much, Aunt Lillie. But perhaps I'll be a doctor."

"Oh no, Sterling. You couldn't be a doctor—you're too tenderhearted. I helped Dr. MacChesney once—when he . . ."

I knew she was remembering the crushed arm of a hired man who had caught his hand in the ensilage cutter. The arm had been amputated on this kitchen table; and Aunt Lillie had administered the chloroform.

"No, perhaps I couldn't be a doctor."

"I think I know what your mother would have wished," Aunt Lillie said. And she looked so much like my mother as she said it that I wondered to whom I was talking in the lamplight of this fog-enshrouded world. I listened as though it were indeed my mother speaking. "I think she would have wanted you to be a writer."

"A writer?"

"And then you could put it all down," Aunt Lillie said, "the way it is now . . . case weather, the fog, the lantern light . . . and the voices of the men—hear them—coming in for breakfast. You could keep it just like this forever."

IX: *March and April*

ARLY in March the first signs of spring began to appear. My woodchucks came up from their holes under the barn to take a cautious look at the world and decided it would be wiser to sleep for a few more weeks. Meadow mice broke through the old snow crust to view the sky; and their big cousins, the muskrats, made similar forays from their ponds and streams to graze on any vegetation which showed a tint of green.

As the mating season approached, the tabby cats mewed and treaded to attract neighborhood toms. Cottontail rabbits thumped the ground, calling for mates. And skunks wandered for miles seeking the consolation that only another skunk can give.

Rascal was becoming restless and unreasonable. On one moonlit night I heard hair-raising screams of rage.

181

Grabbing a flashlight, I went out to find Rascal and another undoubtedly male raccoon trying to get at each other through the chicken wire. I chased away the intruder and put iodine on Rascal's scratches. On another evening I heard very different sounds—the tremolo crooning of an amorous female raccoon trying to reach Rascal for more romantic reasons.

I was only twelve, but not unaware of the meaning of spring. The sighing of the wind through the fur-tipped willows and the disturbing voices of the night made me almost as restless as the other young animals now awakening.

During a week of unseasonably warm weather we put the screens on the windows and doors. On the first night that we left the doors open, Rascal paid me a surprise visit. Evidently he had learned how to lift the hook from the eye on the door of his cage and he had not forgotten how to open the back screen door to the house. He came to my bedroom, chirring happily, and burrowed under the covers.

I could have padlocked the cage, but decided against it. That would have been a grossly unjust reward for Rascal's dexterity and his obvious delight in finding his way to freedom.

However, when on a subsequent night my raccoon raided Reverend Thurman's henhouse, I realized that time was fast running out on our year-long idyl.

Since Christmas I had spent many hours completing my canoe. The most difficult part was stretching and fastening the heavy canvas while the unwieldy fabric was soaking wet. This process did the living room rug a distinct disservice. But I was so pleased with the finished result that my father did not scold me unduly. I asked him to tap the canvas, which had shrunk as tight as a drum over the ribs as it dried. He could see for himself the advantages of nailing it on while wet.

I trimmed the pointed prow and stern with sheet copper, ran a molding around the gunwale, added covered compartments at each end for duffel, and screwed on an outer keel. Except for varnishing the inside and enameling the outside my canoe was ready for service.

"It might be wise to paint it in the barn," my father suggested.

"That seems reasonable," I agreed.

"The green you have chosen will look fine in the water," my father said, "but it doesn't go very well with the other colors in the rug."

The canoe was heavier than I thought it would be, so I asked two very good friends of mine—Art Cunningham, a fishing maniac like myself, and Royal Ladd, who owned a player piano—to help me carry the canoe to the barn, where we mounted it on sawhorses. We worked together on varnishing the smoothly sanded interior and enameling the outside with four coats of glossy green. It was a beautiful thing, that long, streamlined canoe.

The launching was on Saunder's Creek, which had risen many feet above its banks in the spring runoff. In some places the brown flood waters had spread more than a mile in width through the marshes. Art Cunningham and I gave the pencil-slim craft its first workout, skimming over pasture fences, circling into placid backwaters, and streaking down the main current with the ease of a fish or a water bird.

As on the Brule, Rascal rode the prow, fascinated as always by the speed and danger.

Except for the success of the canoe, there was little to be happy about as the season progressed. Reverend Thurman had his shotgun loaded, waiting for one more raid on his henhouse.

Almost as dismaying, Theo and Jessica had finally won their point. We were acquiring a full-time housekeeper whether we wanted one or not. Mrs. Quinn was said to be qualified in every respect: middle-aged, ugly, cranky-clean, and no nonsense. She examined our house minutely, ran her finger over the furniture to show us the dust, and demanded my bedroom for herself.

"That is, if I decide to take the position," Mrs. Quinn added. "I'll let you know in a couple of weeks."

It was sadly apparent that my father would be no match for our new housekeeper. But since we were being allowed two blessed weeks in which to maneuver, I decided to build a second line of defense. The presently unoccupied back bedroom on the second floor was virtually impregnable after I fitted a strong lock on the door and pocketed the key. I explained to my father that I would make my own bed, clean my own room, and let Mrs. Quinn take care of the rest of the place in any way that suited her.

She had expressed herself quite firmly: "No pets in the house!"

I thought that perhaps I might circumvent this unreasonable ruling by preparing a new entrance to my quarters. Opening off the large and airy bedroom was a small study at the very rear of the house. This too would be safeguarded by the lock on the bedroom door. And the little back room furnished another advantage. One window at the end of the gable offered enticing possibilities.

Cutting neat cleats, each eighteen inches in length, I nailed them one above another at convenient intervals up the house to that back window. Now Rascal could climb to see me whenever he wished. I could also conveniently entertain some of my other more-or-less human friends—boys of twelve for the most part.

When I showed my father this new ladder, he merely sighed and suggested that I paint the cleats the same color as the house. I thought this was a brilliant idea since it made them practically invisible. My enemies would never be able to spy them out. In any case they wouldn't know the secret knock: Dum, de, de, dum, dum, DUM DUM, the easily remembered rhythm of "Shave and a Haircut, Six Bits."

With Rascal for my constant companion in all these preparations, I was exhilarated with my stratagems to foil Mrs. Quinn. But deep in my heart I knew that none of these plans would insure Rascal's life. He ran the constant peril of being shot.

Moreover, now that he had grown to young adulthood, he was not entirely happy as a domesticated pet. I realized that I was being selfish and inconsiderate to keep him from his natural life in the woods.

In my prayers I always put Rascal first these days: "Bless Rascal and Daddy and Theo and Jessica and Herschel. And make me a good boy, God, Amen." I suppose I realized that no one needed more protection than my raccoon.

The fourteen days of grace sped by far too swiftly, and the awful moment approached when Mrs. Quinn would confirm her acceptance and move in, bag and baggage. I was certain that she would chase the cats with her broom, flap her apron at the crow, hurt Wowser's feelings by speaking to him sharply, and insist that I padlock Rascal's cage. She had been terrified of my raccoon on the day she had inspected us, and she might become his mortal enemy.

One warm and pleasant Saturday I made my decision. I can remember every detail of that day, hour by hour. Rascal and I had slept in my new bedroom. We came down the fifteen steps of the curved stairway, and ate as usual at the dining room table. Rascal was not behaving well that morning. He walked directly across the tablecloth to the sugar bowl, lifted the lid, and helped himself to two lumps. Thirteen pounds of raccoon on the dining room table is quite a centerpiece. But knowing in my heart what I was plotting, I couldn't scold or slap him.

I told my father that Rascal and I would be away all afternoon and evening on a long canoe ride. I think he knew what I was planning. He looked at us quite sympathetically.

Taking jelly sandwiches, strawberry pop, and more than a pound of soft-shelled pecans, I led Rascal to where my canoe was waiting near the edge of the flooded creek. In a moment it was launched upon the racing stream. All unknowing, my raccoon stood at the prow, occasionally coming back to me for another pecan. I remember thinking that it was sad that Herschel had not come home in time to see my handsome pet.

We floated down the creek, ducking to pass beneath the bridges. Soon we sped out into Rock River, and turned upstream toward Lake Koshkonong. Rascal fell asleep during the hours I labored against the current. He awoke toward sunset as we reached the quiet mirror of the lake itself, heading toward the dark, wild promontory named Koshkonong Point.

It was an evening of full moon, much like the one when I had found my little friend and carried him home in my cap. Rascal was a big, lusty fellow now, thirteen times the weight of the helpless creature to whom I had fed warm milk through a wheat straw. He was very capable in many ways—able to catch all the food he needed along a creek or in a marshy bay. He could climb, swim, and almost talk. As I thought over his accomplishments I was both proud and sad.

We entered the mouth of Koshkonong Creek by moonlight and paddled up this stream several hundred feet into the depths of this wet wilderness. It is a region rich in fish and crayfish, fresh-water clams, muskrats, and mallards—the many forms of life that love wildness and water. The peepers shrilled, and bullfrogs thrummed their bass fid-

dles, and a little screech owl trilled a note reminiscent of Rascal's when he was much younger.

I had decided to let my raccoon make his own decision. But I took off his collar and his leash and put them in a pocket of my corduroy jacket as something to remember him by if he should choose to leave me. We sat together in the canoe, listening to the night sounds all around us, but for *one* sound in particular.

It came at last, the sound I had been waiting for, almost exactly like the crooning tremolo we had heard when the romantic female raccoon had tried to reach him through the chicken wire. Rascal became increasingly excited. Soon he answered with a slightly deeper crooning of his own. The female was now approaching along the edge of the stream, trilling a plaintive call, infinitely tender and questing. Rascal raced to the prow of the canoe, straining to see through the moonlight and shadow, sniffing the air, and asking questions.

"Do as you please, my little raccoon. It's your life," I told him.

He hesitated for a full minute, turned once to look back at me, then took the plunge and swam to the near shore. He had chosen to join that entrancing female somewhere in the shadows. I caught only one glimpse of them in a moonlit glade before they disappeared to begin their new life together.

I left the pecans on a stump near the waterline, hoping Rascal would find them. And I paddled swiftly and desperately away from the place where we had parted.

NEWBERY AWARD BOOKS
AND NEWBERY HONOR BOOKS
AVAILABLE IN PUFFIN

Adam of the Road *by Elizabeth Janet Gray*
Amos Fortune *by Elizabeth Janet Yates*
The Avion My Uncle Flew *by Cyrus Fisher*
Blue Willow *by Doris Gates*
The Corn Grows Ripe *by Dorothy Rhoads*
Daughter of the Mountains *by Louise Rankin*
Dobry *by Monica Shannon*
The Ear, the Eye, and the Arm, *by Nancy Farmer*
Figgs & Phantoms *by Ellen Raskin*
Fog Magic *by Julia L. Sauer*
The Golden Goblet *by Eloise Jarvis McGraw*
The Good Master *written and illustrated by Kate Seredy*
The Hundred Penny Box *by Sharon Bell Mathis*
The Journey Outside *by Mary Q. Steele*
The Light at Tern Rock *by Julia Sauer*
Miss Hickory *by Carolyn Sherwin Bailey*
Moccasin Trail *by Eloise Jarvis McGraw*
My Side of the Mountain *by Jean Craighead George*
The Perilous Gard *by Elizabeth Marie Pope*
Rabbit Hill *written and illustrated by Robert Lawson*
Rascal *by Sterling North*
Red Sails to Capri *by Ann Weil*
The Road From Home *by David Kherdian*
Roller Skates *by Ruth Sawyer*
Roll of Thunder, Hear My Cry *by Mildred D. Taylor*
Tree of Freedom *by Rebecca Caudill*
The Twenty-One Balloons *by William Pène du Bois*
The Secret of the Andes *by Ann Nolan Clark*
The Silver Pencil *by Alice Dagliesh*
The Singing Tree *by Kate Seredy*
A String in the Harp *by Nancy Bond*
The Summer of the Swans *by Betsy Byars*
Upon the Head of the Goat *by Aranka Siegal*
The Westing Game *by Ellen Raskin*
The White Stag *written and illustrated by Kate Seredy*